Creating Dynamic UI with Android Fragments

Leverage the power of Android Fragments to develop
dynamic user interfaces for your apps

Jim Wilson

[PACKT] open source *

community experience distilled

PUBLISHING

BIRMINGHAM - MUMBAI

Creating Dynamic UI with Android Fragments

Copyright © 2013 Packt Publishing

First published: September 2013

Production Reference: 1180913

Published by Packt Publishing Ltd.
Livery Place
35 Livery Street
Birmingham B3 2PB, UK.

ISBN 978-1-78328-309-5

www.packtpub.com

Cover Image by Asher Wishkerman (wishkerman@hotmail.com)

Credits

Author

Jim Wilson

Reviewers

Robert Dale Johnson III

Alex Lockwood

Acquisition Editor

Edward Gordon

Anthony Albuquerque

Commissioning Editor

Poonam Jain

Technical Editors

Pratik More

Anusri Ramchandran

Project Coordinator

Michelle Quadros

Proofreader

Jonathan Todd

Indexer

Priya Subramani

Graphics

Sheetal Aute

Production Coordinator

Kyle Albuquerque

Cover Work

Kyle Albuquerque

About the Author

Jim Wilson is president of JW Hedgehog, Inc., a consulting firm specializing in solutions for the Android, iOS, and Microsoft platforms. Jim has nearly 30 years of software engineering experience, with the past 13 years heavily focused on creating mobile device and location-based solutions. After nearly a decade as a Microsoft Device Application Development MVP, Jim now focuses on developing Android and iOS device applications.

Jim's passion is teaching and mentoring software developers. He is a regular contributor of Android-related training materials to Pluralsight (`http://training.jwhh.com`), a leading provider of online developer training. Jim has authored more than 30 articles on device application development, and has developed mobility and smart client curriculums for several organizations. You can find Jim speaking at a variety of industry conferences, including AnDevCon, Microsoft Professional Developers Conference, Tech Ed, VS Live, Mobile and Embedded Developers Conference, and many others.

Jim and his wife, along with several cats, live in Celebration, Florida (just 3 miles from Walt Disney World). Check out Jim's blog (`http://blog.jwhh.com`) where he talks about a variety of mobile software development issues as well as the fun of life just 3 miles from the "House of Mouse".

You can reach Jim at `androidtraining@jwhh.com`.

Acknowledgments

First and foremost I want to thank my beloved wife, Bonnie. Without her support and patience through the many long nights and six (often seven) day work weeks, this project (and so many others) would never have happened. Our life together has grown into more than I could have ever hoped or dreamed. I love you.

Thank you to my dear friend Rev. Dr. William A. Lewis of Community Presbyterian Church in Celebration. Your friendship and guidance have opened my eyes up to a life of joy and purpose beyond imagination.

To all the folks at Pluralsight, thank you for creating an organization that offers people like me the opportunity to dig deep into technology and share the knowledge gained with others.

About the Reviewers

Robert Dale Johnson III is a Software Engineer who specializes in Android, Joomla, and BD-J (BluRay Disc – Java) development. He graduated in 2008 from California State University Northridge with a BS in Computer Science. He started his career working with BD-J for Deluxe Digital Studios (DDS), Panasonic, and Deluxe Digital Distribution (D3), where he worked on movie titles such as Avatar, Oceans, Spinal Tap, and Conquest of the Planet of the Apes along with many other titles and web-enabled BluRay features. During his time at D3, Robert made the transition from BD-J to Android development where he was a principal developer on the StarzPlay, EncorePlay, and MovieplexPlay apps. He also worked on the NookVideo app developed for non-Nook devices. During his time with D3 Robert moved to Nashville, TN and eventually found Aloompa LLC where he found a home as a Senior Android Developer developing applications for festivals throughout the country such as Coachella, Stagecoach, Governsball, Bannaroo, and many more.

Along with his fulltime professional pursuits, Robert is a seasoned freelancer with many projects in his repertoire (see his personal website www.rdjiii.info) and has started a software consulting company, Contrahere Solutions LLC (see www.contrahere.com). You can reach Robert by going to one of the websites previously mentioned or by e-mail anytime at robert.dale.johnson.iii@gmail.com. Robert is also an avid racquetball player who travels across the country playing in tournaments as a Team Ektelon player. He is a motorcycle enthusiast and loves to dabble in tech such as Arduino and RaspberryPi in his spare time.

I would like to thank my son Xander Johnson for being the best son I could ever wish for. His love and appreciation drives me to become the best that I can, pushing me forward with a smile on my face and joy in my heart. Xander, I love you and thank you for everything you have and will do to make me a better person.

Alex Lockwood is an experienced developer/consultant in the Android community, and an active user on StackOverflow. His blog can be found at http://www.androiddesignpatterns.com.

www.PacktPub.com

Support files, eBooks, discount offers and more

You might want to visit www.PacktPub.com for support files and downloads related to your book.

Did you know that Packt offers eBook versions of every book published, with PDF and ePub files available? You can upgrade to the eBook version at www.PacktPub.com and as a print book customer, you are entitled to a discount on the eBook copy. Get in touch with us at service@packtpub.com for more details.

At www.PacktPub.com, you can also read a collection of free technical articles, sign up for a range of free newsletters and receive exclusive discounts and offers on Packt books and eBooks.

http://PacktLib.PacktPub.com

Do you need instant solutions to your IT questions? PacktLib is Packt's online digital book library. Here, you can access, read and search across Packt's entire library of books.

Why Subscribe?

- Fully searchable across every book published by Packt
- Copy and paste, print and bookmark content
- On demand and accessible via web browser

Free Access for Packt account holders

If you have an account with Packt at www.PacktPub.com, you can use this to access PacktLib today and view nine entirely free books. Simply use your login credentials for immediate access.

Table of Contents

Preface

Long gone are the days of the mobile apps with a static UI squished onto a tiny screen. Today's users expect mobile apps to be dynamic and highly interactive. They expect an app to look fantastic when they're looking at it on their medium-resolution smartphone, and that same app needs to look just as fantastic when they switch over to using it on their high-resolution tablet. Apps need to provide rich navigation features. Also, apps need to be adaptive and responsive.

Trying to meet these demands using Android's traditional activity-centric UI design model is difficult. As developers, we need more control than that afforded by activities. We need a new approach: fragments give us that new approach.

In this book, you'll learn how to use fragments to meet the challenges of creating dynamic UIs in the modern world of mobile app development.

What this book covers

Chapter 1, Fragments and UI Modularization, introduces fragments, UI modularization, and the role fragments play in developing a modularized UI. This chapter demonstrates the creation of simple fragments and using fragments statically within activities.

Chapter 2, Fragments and UI Flexibility, builds on the concepts introduced in the previous chapter to provide solutions to specific differences in device layouts. This chapter explains how to use adaptive activity layout definitions to provide support for a wide variety of device form factors, with a small set of fragments that automatically rearrange based on the current device's UI requirements.

Chapter 3, Fragment Lifecycle and Specialization, discusses the relationship of the lifecycle of fragments to that of activities, and demonstrates the appropriate programming actions at the various points in the lifecycle. Leveraging this knowledge, the special purpose fragment classes `ListFragment` and `DialogFragment` are introduced to demonstrate their behavior and provide a deeper understanding of how their behavior in the activity lifecycle differs from that of standard fragments.

Chapter 4, Working with Fragment Transactions, explains how to create multiple app screens within a single activity, by dynamically adding and removing fragments using fragment transactions. Topics covered include, implementing back button behavior and dynamically adapting multi-fragment UIs to differences in device characteristics.

Chapter 5, Creating Rich Navigation with Fragments, brings everything together by building on the previous chapters to show how to use fragments to enhance the user's experience through rich navigation features. This chapter demonstrates how to implement a number of navigation features, including screen browsing with swipe-based paging, direct screen access with the drop-down list navigation, and random screen viewing with tabs.

What you need for this book

To follow the examples in this book, you should have a basic knowledge of Android programming and a working Android development environment.

This book focuses primarily on Android Studio as the Android development environment, but other tools such as Eclipse with the ADT plugin, JetBrains' IntelliJ IDEA, or a similar Android-enabled development tool can be used.

Who this book is for

This book is for anyone with a basic understanding of Android programming, who would like to improve the appearance and usability of their applications.

Whether you're looking to create a more interactive user experience, create more dynamically adaptive UIs, provide better support for tablets and smartphones in a single app, reduce the complexity of managing your app UIs, or just trying to expand your UI design philosophy, this book is for you.

Conventions

In this book, you will find a number of styles of text that distinguish between different kinds of information. Here are some examples of these styles, and an explanation of their meaning.

Code words in text are shown as follows: "An application initially calls the `startActivity` method to display an instance of `Activity1`. `Activity1`."

A block of code is set as follows:

```
<string-array name="screen_names">
  <item>First View</item>
  <item>Second View</item>
  <item>Third View</item>
</string-array>
```

New terms and **important words** are shown in bold. Words that you see on the screen, in menus or dialog boxes for example, appear in the text like this: "Select **layout** as the **Resource type**."

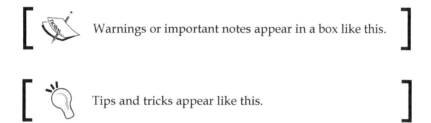

> Warnings or important notes appear in a box like this.

> Tips and tricks appear like this.

Reader feedback

Feedback from our readers is always welcome. Let us know what you think about this book—what you liked or may have disliked. Reader feedback is important for us to develop titles that you really get the most out of.

To send us general feedback, simply send an e-mail to `feedback@packtpub.com`, and mention the book title via the subject of your message.

If there is a topic that you have expertise in and you are interested in either writing or contributing to a book, see our author guide on `www.packtpub.com/authors`.

Customer support

Now that you are the proud owner of a Packt book, we have a number of things to help you to get the most from your purchase.

Downloading the example code

You can download the example code files for all Packt books you have purchased from your account at http://www.packtpub.com. If you purchased this book elsewhere, you can visit http://www.packtpub.com/support and register to have the files e-mailed directly to you.

Errata

Although we have taken every care to ensure the accuracy of our content, mistakes do happen. If you find a mistake in one of our books—maybe a mistake in the text or the code—we would be grateful if you would report this to us. By doing so, you can save other readers from frustration and help us improve subsequent versions of this book. If you find any errata, please report them by visiting http://www.packtpub.com/submit-errata, selecting your book, clicking on the **errata submission form** link, and entering the details of your errata. Once your errata are verified, your submission will be accepted and the errata will be uploaded on our website, or added to any list of existing errata, under the Errata section of that title. Any existing errata can be viewed by selecting your title from http://www.packtpub.com/support.

Piracy

Piracy of copyright material on the Internet is an ongoing problem across all media. At Packt, we take the protection of our copyright and licenses very seriously. If you come across any illegal copies of our works, in any form, on the Internet, please provide us with the location address or website name immediately so that we can pursue a remedy.

Please contact us at copyright@packtpub.com with a link to the suspected pirated material.

We appreciate your help in protecting our authors, and our ability to bring you valuable content.

Questions

You can contact us at questions@packtpub.com if you are having a problem with any aspect of the book, and we will do our best to address it.

1
Fragments and UI Modularization

This chapter introduces fragments, UI modularization, and the role fragments play in developing a modularized UI. The chapter demonstrates creating simple fragments and using fragments statically within activities.

Let us have a look at the topics to be covered:

- The need for UI modularization
- Fragments are the foundation of modularization
- Support for fragments across Android versions
- Creating fragments

By the end of this chapter, we will be able to create and use fragments within a static activity layout.

The need for a new approach to UI creation

Chances are that the first class you learned to use when you became an Android developer was the `Activity` class. After all, the `Activity` class provided your app with a user interface. By organizing your user interface components onto an activity, the activity became the canvas on which you were painting your application masterpiece.

In the early days of Android, building an application's user interface directly within an activity worked reasonably well. The majority of early applications had a relatively simple user interface and the number of different Android device form factors was small. In most cases, with the help of a few layout resources, a single activity worked fine across different device form factors.

Today, Android devices come in a wide variety of form factors with incredible variation in their size and shape. Combine this with the rich, highly interactive user interfaces of modern Android applications, and the creation of a single activity that effectively manages the user interface across such divergent form factors becomes extremely difficult.

A possible solution is to define one activity to provide the user experience for a subset of device form factors; for example, smartphones. Then define another activity for a different subset of form factors such as tablets. The problem with this approach is that activities tend to have a lot of responsibilities beyond simply rendering the user interface. With multiple activities performing essentially the same tasks, we must either duplicate the logic within each of the activities, or increase the complexity of our program by finding ways to share the logic across the activities. The approach of using different activities for different form factors also substantially increases the number of activities in the program, easily doubling or tripling the number of activities required.

We need a better solution. We need a solution that allows us to modularize our application user interface into sections that we can arrange as needed within an activity. Fragments are that solution.

Android fragments allow us to partition the user interface into functional groupings of user interface components and logic. An activity can load and arrange the fragments as needed for a given device form factor. The fragments take care of the form factor details while the activity manages the overall user interface issues.

The broad platform support of fragments

The `Fragment` class was added to Android at API Level 11 (Android 3.0). This was the first version of Android that officially supported tablets. The addition of tablet support exacerbated an already difficult problem; developing Android applications was becoming increasingly difficult because of the wide variety of Android device form factors.

Fortunately, fragments provide a solution to the problem. With fragments, we can much more easily create applications that support a variety of form factors, because we can partition our user interfaces into effective groupings of components and their associated logic.

There was one problem with fragments. Up until very recently, the majority of Android devices had an API Level below 11 and therefore didn't support fragments. Fortunately, Google released the Android Support Library, available at `http://developer.android.com/tools/extras/support-library.html`, which makes fragments available to any device running API Level 4 (Android 1.6) or above. With the Android Support Library, fragments are now available to virtually every Android device in use.

Applications created with Android Studio automatically include the Android Support Library, and therefore support fragments on virtually all SDK versions in use. If you will be using a development tool other than Android Studio to create applications that target devices running on a SDK level below 11, see the Android Developers Blog post, *Fragments For All*, available at `http://android-developers. blogspot.com/2011/03/fragments-for-all.html`, for directions on manually adding the Android Support Library to your projects.

Fragments simplify common Android tasks

Fragments not only simplify the way we create our application user interfaces but they also simplify many of the built-in Android user interface tasks. User interface concepts such as tabbed displays, list displays, and dialog boxes have all historically had distinctly different approaches. When we think about it, though, they are all variations on a common concept, that is, combining user interface components and logic into a functional group. Fragments formalize this concept, and therefore allow us to take a consistent approach to these formerly disparate tasks. We talk about each of these issues in detail as well as some of the specialized fragment classes such as the `DialogFragment` class and the `ListFragment` class later in this book.

The relationship between fragments and activities

Fragments do not replace activities but rather supplement them. A fragment always exists within an activity. An activity instance can contain any number of fragments but a given fragment instance can only exist within a single activity. A fragment is closely tied to the activity on which it exists and the lifetime of that fragment is tightly coupled to the lifetime of the containing activity. We'll talk much more about the close relationship between the lifetime of a fragment and the containing activity in *Chapter 3, Fragment Lifecycle and Specialization*.

One thing we don't want to do is make the common mistake of overusing fragments. So often when someone learns about fragments, they make the assumption that every activity must contain fragments, and that's simply not the case.

As we go through this book, we'll discuss the features and capabilities of fragments and a variety of scenarios where they work well. We'll always want to keep those in mind as we're building our applications. In those situations where fragments add value, we definitely want to use them. However, it is equally important that we avoid complicating our applications by using fragments in those cases where they do not provide value.

Making the shift to fragments

Although fragments are a very powerful tool, fundamentally they do something very simple. Fragments group user interface components and their associated logic. Creating the portion of your user interface associated with a fragment is very much like doing so for an activity. In most cases, the view hierarchy for a particular fragment is created from a layout resource; although, just as with activities, the view hierarchy can be programmatically generated.

Creating a layout resource for a fragment follows the same rules and techniques as doing so for an activity. The key difference is that we're looking for opportunities to partition our user interface layout into manageable subsections when working with fragments.

The easiest way to get started working with fragments is for us to walk through converting a traditional activity-oriented user interface to use fragments.

The old thinking – activity-oriented

To get started, let's first look at the appearance and structure of the application we're going to convert. This application contains a single activity that, when run, looks like the following screenshot:

The activity displays a list of five book titles in the top portion of the activity. When the user selects one of those books titles, the description of that book appears in the bottom portion of the activity.

Defining the activity appearance

The appearance of the activity is defined in a layout resource file named `activity_main.xml` that contains the following layout description:

```xml
<LinearLayout
    xmlns:android="http://schemas.android.com/apk/res/android"
    android:orientation="vertical"
    android:layout_width="match_parent"
    android:layout_height="match_parent">

    <!-- List of Book Titles -->
    <ScrollView
        android:layout_width="match_parent"
        android:layout_height="0dp"
        android:id="@+id/scrollTitles"
        android:layout_weight="1">
    <RadioGroup
        android:id="@+id/bookSelectGroup"
        android:layout_height="wrap_content"
        android:layout_width="wrap_content"
    >
        <RadioButton
            android:id="@+id/dynamicUiBook"
            android:layout_height="wrap_content"
            android:layout_width="wrap_content"
            android:text="@string/dynamicUiTitle"
            android:checked="true" />
        <RadioButton
            android:id="@+id/android4NewBook"
            android:layout_height="wrap_content"
            android:layout_width="wrap_content"
            android:text="@string/android4NewTitle" />

        <!-- Other RadioButtons elided for clarify -->

    </RadioGroup>
    </ScrollView>

    <!-- Description of selected book -->
    <ScrollView
        android:layout_width="match_parent"
        android:layout_height="0dp"
        android:id="@+id/scrollDescription"
```

```
        android:layout_weight="1">

    <TextView
        android:layout_width="wrap_content"
        android:layout_height="wrap_content"
        android:textAppearance="?android:attr/
          textAppearanceMedium"
        android:text="@string/dynamicUiDescription"
        android:id="@+id/textView"
        android:paddingLeft="@dimen/activity_horizontal_margin"
        android:paddingRight="@dimen/activity_horizontal_margin"
        android:gravity="fill_horizontal"/>
    </ScrollView>
</LinearLayout>
```

Downloading the example code

You can download the example code files for all Packt books you have purchased from your account at http://www.packtpub.com. If you purchased this book elsewhere, you can visit http://www.packtpub. com/support and register to have the files e-mailed directly to you.

This layout resource is reasonably simple and is explained as follows:

- The overall layout is defined within a vertically-oriented LinearLayout element containing the two ScrollView elements

- Both of the ScrollView elements have a layout_weight value of 1 that causes the top-level LinearLayout element to divide the screen equally between the two ScrollView elements

- The top ScrollView element, with the id value of scrollTitles, wraps a RadioGroup element containing a series of the RadioButton elements, one for each book

- The bottom ScrollView element, with the id value of scrollDescription, contains a TextView element that displays the selected book's description

Displaying the activity UI

The application's activity class, MainActivity, inherits directly from the android.app.Activity class. To display the activity's user interface, we override the onCreate method and call the setContentView method passing the R.layout.activity_main layout resource ID.

```java
public class MainActivity extends Activity {

  @Override
  protected void onCreate(Bundle savedInstanceState) {
    super.onCreate(savedInstanceState);
    // load the activity_main layout resource
    setContentView(R.layout.activity_main);
  }

  // Other methods elided for clarity
}
```

The new thinking – fragment-oriented

The activity-oriented user interface we currently have would be fine if all Android devices had the same form factor. As we've discussed, that's not the case.

We need to partition the application user interface so that we can switch to a fragment-oriented approach. With proper partitioning, we can be ready to make some simple enhancements to our application to help it adapt to device differences.

Let's look at some simple changes we can make that will partition our user interface.

Creating the fragment layout resources

The first step in moving to a fragment-oriented user interface is to identify the natural partitions in the existing user interface. In the case of this application, the natural partitions are reasonably easy to identify. The list of book titles is one good candidate, and the book description is the other. We'll make them each a separate fragment.

Defining the layout as a reusable list

For the list of book titles, we have the option to define the fragment to contain either the ScrollView element that's nearest to the top (has an id value of scrollTitles) or just the RadioGroup element within that ScrollView element. When creating a fragment, we want to structure it such that the fragment is most easily reused. Although the RadioGroup element is all we need to display the list of titles, it seems likely that we'll always want the user to be able to scroll the list of titles if necessary. With this being the case, it makes sense to include the ScrollView element in this fragment.

To create a fragment for the book list, we define a new layout resource file called `fragment_book_list.xml`. We copy the top `ScrollView` element and its contents from the `activity_main.xml` resource file to the `fragment_book_list.xml` resource file. The resulting `fragment_book_list.xml` resource file is as follows:

```
<!-- List of Book Titles -->
<ScrollView
    android:layout_width="match_parent"
    android:layout_height="0dp"
    android:id="@+id/scrollTitles"
    android:layout_weight="1">
  <RadioGroup
      android:id="@+id/bookSelectGroup "
      android:layout_height="wrap_content"
      android:layout_width="wrap_content" >
    <RadioButton
        android:id="@+id/dynamicUiBook"
        android:layout_height="wrap_content"
        android:layout_width="wrap_content"
        android:text="@string/dynamicUiTitle"
        android:checked="true"    />
    <RadioButton
        android:id="@+id/android4NewBook"
        android:layout_height="wrap_content"
        android:layout_width="wrap_content"
        android:text="@string/android4NewTitle"    />

    <!-- Other RadioButtons elided for clarify -->

  </RadioGroup>
</ScrollView>
```

This gives us a layout resource consistent with the book title portion of the user interface as it appeared in the activity layout resource. This is a good start.

Minimize assumptions

An effective fragment-oriented user interface is constructed with layout resources that minimize assumptions about where and how the fragment is used. The fewer assumptions we make about a fragment's use, the more reusable the fragment becomes.

The layout in the `fragment_book_list.xml` resource file as we now have it is very limiting because it includes significant assumptions. For example, the root `ScrollView` element includes a `layout_height` attribute with a value of `0`. This assumes that the fragment will be placed within a layout that calculates the height for the fragment.

A `layout_height` attribute value of `0` prevents the `ScrollView` element from properly rendering when we use the fragment within any of the many layouts that require the `ScrollView` element to specify a meaningful height. A `layout_height` attribute value of `0` prevents the fragment from properly rendering even when doing something as simple as placing the fragment within a horizontally oriented `LinearLayout` element. The `layout_weight` attribute has similar issues.

In general, a good practice is to design the fragment to fully occupy whatever space it is placed within. This gives the layout in which the fragment is used the most control over the placement and sizing of the fragment.

To do this, we'll remove the `layout_weight` attribute from the `ScrollView` element and change the `layout_height` attribute value to `match_parent`. Because the `ScrollView` element is now the root node of the layout resource, we also need to add the `android` namespace prefix declaration.

The following code snippet shows the updated `ScrollView` element:

```
<ScrollView
    xmlns:android="http://schemas.android.com/apk/res/android"
    android:layout_width="match_parent"
    android:layout_height="match_parent"
    android:id="@+id/scrollTitles">

  <!--RadioGroup and RadioButton elements elided for clarity -->

</ScrollView>
```

With the updated `ScrollView` element, the fragment layout can now adapt to almost any layout it's referenced within.

Encapsulating the display layout

For the book description, we'll define a layout resource file called
`fragment_book_desc.xml`. The fragment layout includes the contents
of the activity layout resource's bottom `ScrollView` element (has an `id`
value of `scrollDescription`). Just as in the book list fragment,
we'll remove the `layout_weight` attribute, set the `layout_height`
attribute to `match_parent`, and add the `android` namespace
prefix declaration.

The `fragment_book_desc.xml` layout resource file appears as follows:

```xml
<!-- Description of selected book -->
<ScrollView
    xmlns:android="http://schemas.android.com/apk/res/android"
    android:layout_width="match_parent"
    android:layout_height="match_parent"
    android:id="@+id/scrollDescription">
  <TextView
      android:layout_width="wrap_content"
      android:layout_height="wrap_content"
      android:textAppearance="?android:attr/textAppearanceMedium"
      android:text="@string/dynamicUiDescription"
      android:id="@+id/textView"
      android:paddingLeft="@dimen/activity_horizontal_margin"
      android:paddingRight="@dimen/activity_horizontal_margin"
      android:gravity="fill_horizontal"/>
</ScrollView>
```

Creating the Fragment class

Just like when creating an activity, we need more than a simple layout definition for
our fragment; we also need a class.

Wrapping the list in a fragment

All fragment classes must extend the `android.app.Fragment` class either directly
or indirectly.

> For projects that rely on the Android Support Library to provide
> fragment support for pre-API Level 11 (Android 3.0) devices, use
> the `android.support.v4.app.Fragment` class in place of the
> `android.app.Fragment` class.

We'll call the class for the fragment that manages the book list, BookListFragment. The class will directly extend the Fragment class as follows:

```
Import android.app.Ftragment;
public class BookListFragment extends Fragment { … }
```

During the creation of a fragment, the Android framework calls a number of methods on that fragment. One of the most important of these is the onCreateView method. The onCreateView method is responsible for returning the view hierarchy represented by the fragment. The Android framework attaches that returned view hierarchy for the fragment to the appropriate place in the activity's overall view hierarchy.

In a case like the BookListFragment class where the Fragment class inherits directly from the Fragment class, we must override the onCreateView method and perform the work necessary to construct the view hierarchy.

The onCreateView method receives three parameters. We'll focus on just the first two for now:

- inflater: This is a reference to a LayoutInflater instance that is able to read and expand layout resources within the context of the containing activity

- container: This is a reference to the ViewGroup instance within the activity's layout where the fragment's view hierarchy is to be attached

The LayoutInflater class provides a method called inflate that handles the details of converting a layout resource into the corresponding view hierarchy and returns a reference to the root view of that hierarchy. Using the LayoutInflater.inflate method, we can implement our BookListFragment class' onCreateView method to construct and return the view hierarchy corresponding to the R.layout.fragment_book_list layout resource as shown in the following code:

```
@Override
public View onCreateView(LayoutInflater inflater, ViewGroup
container, Bundle savedInstanceState) {
    View viewHierarchy =
    inflater.inflate(R.layout.fragment_book_list,
    container, false);
    return viewHierarchy;
}
```

You'll notice in the preceding code we include the `container` reference and a Boolean value of `false` in the call to the `inflate` method. The `container` reference provides the necessary layout parameters for the `inflate` method to properly format the new view hierarchy. The parameter value of `false` indicates that `container` is to be used only for the layout parameters. If this value were true, the `inflate` method would also attach the new view hierarchy to the `container` view group. We do not want to attach the new view hierarchy to the `container` view group in the `onCreateView` method because the activity will handle that.

Providing the display fragment

For the book description fragment, we'll define a class called `BookDescFragment`. This class is identical to the `BookListFragment` class except the `BookDescFragment` class uses the `R.layout.fragment_book_desc` layout resource as follows:

```
public class BookDescFragment extends Fragment {
  @Override
  public View onCreateView(LayoutInflater inflater, ViewGroup
    container, Bundle savedInstanceState) {
    View viewHierarchy =
      inflater.inflate(R.layout.fragment_book_desc, container,
        false);
    return viewHierarchy;
  }
}
```

Converting the activity to use fragments

With the fragments defined, we can now update the activity to use them. To get started, we'll remove all the book titles and description layout information from the `activity_main.xml` layout resource file. The file now contains just the top-level `LinearLayout` element and comments to show where the book titles and description belong as follows:

```
<LinearLayout
    android:orientation="vertical"
    android:layout_width="match_parent"
    android:layout_height="match_parent"
    xmlns:android="http://schemas.android.com/apk/res/android">

  <!-- List of Book Titles  -->

  <!-- Description of selected book  -->

</LinearLayout>
```

Using the `fragment` element, we can add a fragment to the layout by referencing the fragment's class name with the `name` attribute. For example, we reference the book list fragment's class, `BookListFragment`, as follows:

```
<fragment
    android:name="com.jwhh.fragments.BookListFragment"
    android:id="@+id/fragmentTitles"/>
```

We want our activity user interface to appear the same using fragments as it did before we converted it to use fragments. To do this, we add the same `layout_width`, `layout_height`, and `layout_weight` attribute values to the fragment elements as were on the `ScrollView` elements in the original layout.

With that, the complete layout resource file for the activity, `activity_main.xml`, now looks like the following code:

```
<LinearLayout
    android:orientation="vertical"
    android:layout_width="match_parent"
    android:layout_height="match_parent"
    xmlns:android="http://schemas.android.com/apk/res/android">

  <!-- List of Book Titles -->
  <fragment
      android:layout_width="match_parent"
      android:layout_height="0dp"
      android:layout_weight="1"
      android:name="com.jwhh.fragments.BookListFragment"
      android:id="@+id/fragmentTitles"/>

  <!-- Description of selected book -->
  <fragment
      android:layout_width="match_parent"
      android:layout_height="0dp"
      android:layout_weight="1"
      android:name="com.jwhh.fragments.BookDescFragment"
      android:id="@+id/fragmentDescription"/>
</LinearLayout>
```

If you are working with Android Studio, you might find a tools:layout attribute on the fragment element. This attribute is used by Android Studio to provide a preview of the layout within the graphical designer. It has no effect on your application's appearance when the application is run.

When the application is run, the user interface will now appear exactly as it did when it was defined entirely within the activity. If we're targeting Android devices running API Level 11 (Android 3.0) or later, there is no need to make any changes to the Activity class because the Activity class is simply loading and displaying the layout resource at this point.

Activities and backward compatibility

When using the Android Support Library to provide pre-API Level 11 (Android 3.0) fragment support, we have one additional step. In this case, we have to make one small, but important change to our activity. We must change the MainActivity class' base class from the Activity class to the android.support.v4.app.FragmentActivity class. Because the pre-API Level 11 Activity class doesn't understand fragments, we use the FragmentActivity class from the Android Support Library to add fragment support to our MainActivity class.

Summary

The shift from the old thinking of being activity-oriented to the new thinking of being fragment-oriented opens our applications up to rich possibilities. Fragments allow us to better organize both the appearance of the user interface and the code we use to manage it. With fragments, our application user interface has a more modular approach that frees us from being tied to the specific capabilities of a small set of devices and prepares us to work with the rich devices of today, and the wide variety of new devices to come tomorrow.

In the next chapter, we'll build on the modularized user interface we've created with fragments to enable our application to automatically adapt to differences in the various device form factors with only minimal changes to our application.

2
Fragments and UI Flexibility

This chapter builds on the concepts introduced in the previous chapter to provide solutions to addressing specific differences in device layouts. The chapter explains the use of adaptive Activity layout definitions to create apps that automatically rearrange their user interface in response to differences in device form factors. With adaptive Activity layout definitions, applications are able to support a wide variety of devices using just a few properly designed fragments.

In this chapter, we will cover the following topics:

- Simplifying the challenge of supporting device differences
- Dynamic resource selection
- Coordinating fragment content
- The role of `FragmentManager`
- Supporting fragments across activities

By the end of this chapter, we will be able to implement a user interface that uses fragments to automatically adapt to differences in device layouts and coordinates user actions across the involved fragments.

Creating UI flexibility

Utilizing fragments in our user interface design provides a good foundation for creating applications that more easily adapt to device differences, but we must go a little further to create truly flexible UIs. We must design our application such that the fragments that make up the UI are easily rearranged in response to the characteristics of the device on which the app is currently running.

To achieve this, we must use some techniques to dynamically change the layout of individual fragments in response to the current device's characteristics. Once we employ such a technique, we must be sure that we implement our fragments in such a way that each fragment is able to function effectively independent of layout changes that might affect the behavior or even existence of other fragments within the activity.

Dynamic fragment layout selection

As we mentioned in the previous section, creating a flexible UI requires that the layout and positioning of fragments within an activity must be able to change in response to differences in device characteristics. We can include code in our application to dynamically arrange fragments in response to the form factor of the device on which our app is running, but in most cases, doing so is not only unnecessary but also undesirable. The deeper the dependencies between the user interface and application code, the more difficult maintaining and enhancing an application becomes. Although there will always be some degree of dependency between our user interface and application code, we want to minimize such dependencies and instead do as much of our user interface layout-related work within layout resources as possible.

The easiest way to build flexibility into our application user interface is to take advantage of the Android resource system's built-in device adaptability. Android allows us to design different layout-related resources for our application with each optimized for and associated with a specific set of device characteristics. At runtime, the Android resource system takes care of automatically selecting and loading the appropriate resources for the current device. Although this feature can be used to dynamically modify the layout of any activity, we'll see that it is particularly effective when used in conjunction with fragments.

To see Android resource selection in action, let's continue with our application from the previous chapter. As you'll recall, the layout for our activity is in the `activity_main.xml` resource file and looks like this:

```
<LinearLayout
    android:orientation=""vertical""
    android:layout_width=""match_parent""
    android:layout_height=""match_parent""
    xmlns:android=""http://schemas.android.com/apk/res/android"">

    <!-- List of Book Titles -->
    <fragment
        android:layout_width=""match_parent""
        android:layout_height=""0dp""
```

```
        android:layout_weight=""1""
        android:name=""com.jwhh.fragments.BookListFragment""
        android:id=""@+id/fragmentTitles""/>

    <!-- Description of selected book -->
    <fragment
        android:layout_width=""match_parent""
        android:layout_height=""0dp""
        android:layout_weight=""1""
        android:name=""com.jwhh.fragments.BookDescFragment""
        android:id=""@+id/fragmentDescription""/>
</LinearLayout>
```

This layout stacks our fragments, BookListFragment and BookDescFragment, one on top of the other. Although that layout renders well on a smartphone held vertically in the portrait orientation, rotating the phone so that it's held horizontally in the landscape orientation creates a much less attractive appearance as seen here:

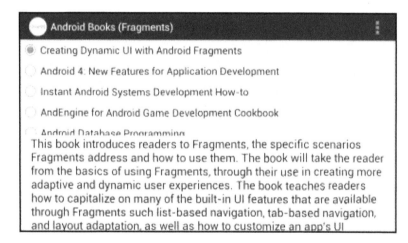

The current layout is clearly not making the best use of the available screen space in this orientation. When the phone is orientated in landscape, the application would look much better if we position the two fragments side-by-side.

Adding an alternate layout resource

We can add support for an alternative layout to our application by creating a new resource file with the fragments appropriately arranged. To create the resource file, we first add another folder under the `res` folder of the project tree called `layout-land`.

 The resource folder name creates the association between the resource file and the device characteristics, not any special behavior on the part of Android Studio.

To create the new folder in Android Studio, perform the following steps:

1. Expand the **src** folder in the project explorer window.
2. Expand the **main** folder under **src**.
3. Right-click on the **res** folder under **main**.
4. Select **New**.
5. Select **Android resource directory** to open the **New Resource Directory** dialog.
6. Select **layout** as **Resource type:**.
7. Highlight **Orientation** under **Available qualifiers:** and click on the **>>** button to move it to **Chosen qualifiers:**.
8. Select **Landscape** under **Screen orientation:**.

The **New Resource Directory** dialog will appear similar to the following screenshot:

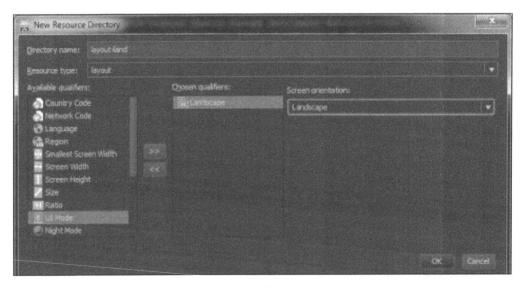

Now copy the `activity_main.xml` resource file from the **layout** resource folder to the **layout-land** resource folder. We now have two copies of the `activity_main.xml` resource file as shown in the following screenshot:

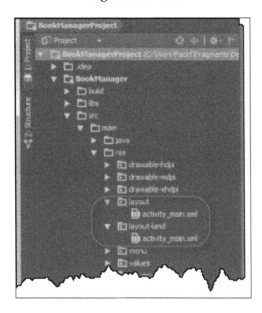

We can now modify the `activity_main.xml` resource file in the `layout-land` folder to arrange the fragments to render properly when the phone is in landscape orientation. First, we switch the `LinearLayout` element from a vertical to a horizontal orientation. We then change the `layout_width` values for each fragment to `0dp` and the `layout_height` values to `match_parent`. We can leave each of the fragment's `layout_weight` value as 1 so that `LinearLayout` spaces them equally left to right.

The updated resource file looks like this:

```
<LinearLayout
    android:orientation=""horozontal""
    android:layout_width=""match_parent""
    android:layout_height=""match_parent""
    xmlns:android=""http://schemas.android.com/apk/res/android"">

<!-- List of Book Titles -->
<fragment
    android:layout_width=""0dp""
    android:layout_height="" match_parent""
    android:layout_weight=""1""
    android:name=""com.jwhh.fragments.BookListFragment""
    android:id=""@+id/fragmentTitles""/>

<!-- Description of selected book -->
```

```
<fragment
    android:layout_width=""0dp""
    android:layout_height=""match_parent""
    android:layout_weight=""1""
    android:name=""com.jwhh.fragments.BookDescFragment""
    android:id=""@+id/fragmentDescription""/>
</LinearLayout>
```

Having done nothing more than adding this simple resource file to our project, the application now displays the list of titles and book description next to one another when run on a device held in a landscape orientation as shown in the following screenshot:

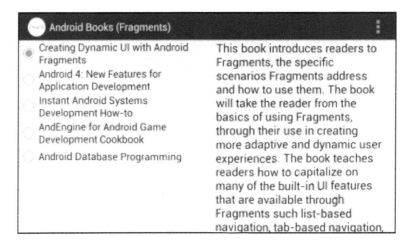

During runtime, when the MainActivity class loads the R.layout.activity_main resource, the Android resource system returns the appropriate version of the activity_main.xml resource file for that orientation. When the user rotates the device to a different orientation, Android automatically recreates the activity and loads the appropriate resource for the new orientation.

The Android environment detects a wide variety of device form factor characteristics. By taking advantage of fragments, we are able to create an application that easily adapts to device differences by simply providing different layout resource files that shift around the location of our fragments as if they are puzzle pieces.

Without fragments, we would've had to provide the entire layout for the activity, radio buttons, text views, everything, in both of the layout files. We would then find ourselves having to maintain two complex, almost identical files. By using fragments, the individual pieces are self-contained and non-duplicated. Fragments modify the layout in an easy manner and simplify our application maintenance.

Managing fragment layout by screen size

The same technique we use to adapt our user interface to device orientation differences can be taken much further to work with differences in screen size. The Android resource system has device screen size awareness and therefore supports creating corresponding resource folders. The resource selection can be based on general screen size groups or specific screen size constraints.

Differences in device screen size are one of the most common reasons for using layout resources to manage fragments. With this being the case, understanding how to use layout resources to deal with differences in screen size is essential to working effectively with fragments.

Resource screen size groups

The configuration information of each Android device includes the screen size group to which the device belongs. The four screen size groups are small, normal, large, or xlarge.

 For specific information on the size of screens in each group, see *Range of screens supported* in the Android documentation available at `http://developer.android.com/guide/ practices/screens_support.html#range`.

Just as we created a specific layout resource file for landscape orientation, we can create a layout resource file targeting a particular screen size group. We associate the resource file with the desired screen size group by placing the file in the appropriately named resource folder. For example, we place a layout resource file designed for devices with a screen size group of large in the `layout-large` resource folder.

Screen size groups date back to the early days of Android when there was little practical experience in dealing with the wide variety of device form factors that now exist. As time has gone on and the number of Android device form factors has grown, file size groups have turned out to be a less than ideal solution. Problems with screen size groups stem from two main issues:

1. The size range of the groups is not consistently applied, which results in the size range within the groups overlapping one another. One device with a 7-inch screen might be classified as large while another device with the same size screen might be classified as xlarge.

2. Groups are sometimes too broad. For example, the large group includes devices with 5-inch screens and devices with 7-inch screens. These screen sizes tend to have very different layout requirements. A device with a 5-inch screen tends to work best with handset-style layouts like that for a smartphone, whereas a device with a 7-inch screen tends to work best with a tablet-style layout.

Size groups are still in use because they are the best option available for dealing with screen size differences on pre-API Level 13 devices. Fortunately, less than half of the Android devices in use today are pre-API Level 13, and the ratio is shrinking rapidly.

 For information on the distribution of devices in use by API Level or by screen size group, see the Android developer, *Dashboards*, available at `http://developer.android.com/about/dashboards`.

Resource screen size qualifiers

At API Level 13 (Android 3.2), Android introduced a substantial improvement over screen size groups known as resource screen size qualifiers. Resource screen size qualifiers allow us to associate resources with specific screen size requirements. With screen size qualifiers, we have a very detailed level of control over which layout resources are associated with each device form factor.

To avoid the complications inherent in the wide variety of screen pixel densities and physical screen sizes available, Android uses a canonicalized unit of measure called the **density independent pixel** (**dp**) when managing screen sizes. If you've been working with Android for any length of time, you are probably already familiar with density independent pixels as they are the preferred unit of measure when positioning and sizing views within an Android user interface.

A dp always corresponds to the physical size of a pixel on a 160 dpi device and therefore provides a consistent unit of measure independent of the physical pixel size of the device. For example, one 7-inch display device may have a physical pixel count of 1280x720 while another 7-inch display device has a physical pixel count of 1920x1080, but both devices have a dp count of approximately 1000x600. The Android platform takes care of the details of mapping between density independent pixels and the physical pixels of a device.

Android provides three types of screen size qualifiers: smallest width, available screen width, and available screen height:

- **Smallest width screen size qualifier:** This is referred to as smallest screen width in the Android Studio New Directory Resource dialog. It corresponds to the number of device independent pixels at the screen's narrowest point independent of the device orientation. Changing the device orientation does not change the device's smallest width. We specify the name of a resource folder based on the device's smallest width by adding `sw`, followed by the desired screen size in device independent pixels, followed by `dp`. For example, a layout resource folder containing layout resource files for devices with a smallest width of at least 600 dp is named `layout-sw600dp`.

- **Available width screen size qualifier:** This is referred to as screen width in the Android Studio New Directory Resource dialog. It corresponds to the number of device independent pixels measured left to right at the device's current orientation. Changing the device orientation changes the available width. We specify the name of a resource folder based on available width by adding `w`, followed by the width in density independent pixels, followed by `dp`. A layout resource folder containing resource files for a device with an available width of at least 600 dp is named `layout-w600dp`.

- **Available height screen size qualifier:** This is referred to as screen height in the Android Studio New Directory Resource dialog. It corresponds to the number of device independent pixels measured top to bottom, but otherwise behaves identically to the available width screen size qualifier, and follows the same naming pattern except that `h` is used instead of `w`. A layout resource folder containing resource files for a device with an available height of at least 600 dp is named `layout-h600dp`.

Eliminating redundancy

As the number of form factors our application targets grow, managing the resource files within the different layout resource folders can become somewhat complicated due to the fact that we'll likely want to use the same layout resource file for different qualifiers. To demonstrate this problem, let's update our application to use the version of the `activity_main.xml` resource file we currently use for landscape-oriented devices on other devices. We'll use that same resource file on devices in the large screen size group and on devices with a current width of 600 dp or greater.

We first create two additional folders under our `res` folder: `layout-large` and `layout-w600dp`. We then copy the `activity_main.xml` file from the `layout-land` folder to the two folders we just created. Doing this is easy enough but we now have a maintenance headache. Every time we make a change to that layout, we have to be sure that we make it in all three folders.

To avoid this resource file duplication, we can use layout aliasing.

Layout aliasing

Layout aliasing allows us to have just a single copy of each layout resource file. We can then provide the resource system with information as to which file to choose for each form factor.

To get started, we'll rename the `activity_main.xml` resource file in the `layout-land` resource folder as `activity_main_wide.xml`. We then move the file to the `layout` resource folder and delete the `layout-land` folder.

We now create a new resource folder called `values-land` under the `res` folder. To create the folder in Android Studio, follow the same steps as we used earlier to create the `layout-land` folder except set the **Resource type:** as **values** rather than **layout**.

Within this folder, we create a new resource file, the name of which doesn't matter, but the file containing values for aliasing is often named `refs.xml` because it contains a list of references to other resources, so that's what we'll use. To create the file using Android Studio, perform the following steps:

1. Right-click on the **values-land** resource folder.
2. Select **New**.
3. Select the **values** resource file.
4. Specify `refs.xml` as the filename.

In the `refs.xml` file, be sure that there is already a root element named `resources`. Within that element, add an `item` element with a `type` attribute value of `layout`. This indicates that we're providing an alias entry for a layout resource. We set the value of the `name` attribute to be the name of the default layout resource, which in our case is `activity_main`. We then give the `item` element a value of `@layout/activity_main_wide`. The complete `refs.xml` resource file now appears as follows:

```
<resources>
  <item type=""layout"" name=""activity_main"">
    @layout/activity_main_wide
  </item>
</resources>
```

With this file in place, any call to load the layout resource R.layout.activity_main will instead load R.layout.activity_main_wide when the application is running on a device in landscape orientation.

To add support for devices in the large group and those with a current width of at least 600 dp, we simply create two more resource folders, values-large and values-w600dp, and copy the refs.xml file from the values-land folder to each. The layout and values resource folders now appear as shown in the following screenshot:

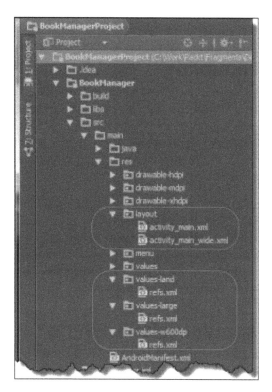

We now have support for all the desired form factors with no unnecessary duplication of layout resource files. We do have duplication of the refs.xml file, but it's a much simpler file than the layout resource file and is less likely to change.

See *Table 2* of the Android *Providing Resources* guide for the order of precedence Android follows when performing layout aliasing, available at http://developer.android.com/guide/topics/resources/providing-resources.html.

Design fragments for flexibility

With our user interface well-partitioned and adaptable, we need to be sure that each fragment functions effectively, as layout differences cause the behavior and possibly even the existence of other fragments within the activity to change. When an application user interface is divided into fragments, the fragments exist completely independent of one another rarely. Very often a user's interaction with one fragment has some effect on other fragments within the same activity. In the case of our application, this issue arises when a user selects a book within BookListFragment. In response to the user's selection, the application is responsible for displaying the corresponding description in BookDescFragment.

Avoiding tight coupling

One possible solution to coordinating fragment content is to allow the fragments to directly communicate with one another. To coordinate content within our application, we could pass the BookDescFragment reference into BookListFragment when we first create the activity. In response to each user selection within BookListFragment, BookListFragment would then directly update TextView contained within BookDescFragment.

Although simple to implement, this solution is problematic because it tightly couples the two Fragment classes to each other. The BookListFragment fragment is only usable within activities that also contain the BookDescFragment fragment, and making changes to the layout of BookDescFragment may potentially break BookListFragment. We always want to keep in mind that a key goal of using fragments is to be well-partitioned and adaptable.

Abstracting fragment relationships

Instead of creating direct relationships between the fragments, we can take advantage of the abstraction provided by interfaces. By defining a simple callback interface to represent the act of a user making a book selection, we can completely eliminate tight coupling between fragments. The BookListFragment class can be written to provide notification of a user selection through the interface. By implementing the interface on the activity, the activity can then handle coordinating the user selection within BookListFragment with updating the displayed description within BookDeskFragment.

Defining the callback interface

The callback interface should include methods for any interaction with the fragment that may be meaningful to the activity containing the fragment. At the same time, the interface should not burden the activity with unnecessary details. The interface should be focused on application-level actions such as selecting a book rather than implementation-level actions such as tapping on a radio button. The implementation-level details should be isolated within the fragment. We should also be sure to design the interface without any preconceived ideas of what the activity will do with the notification.

In the case of `BookListFragment`, the only action of interest to the activity is the user selecting a book. This tells us the interface needs just a single method; we'll call the interface method `onSelectedBookChanged`. We know in the case of this application, the goal is to display the selected book description, so one possibility is to have the `onSelectedBookChanged` method include a parameter for the book description. The problem with passing the book description is that doing so limits the use of `BookListFragment` to just this one use case, displaying the book description. Instead, by passing an identifier for the book, `BookListFragment` is available for any use case in which the user selects a book. For simplicity, in our example, we'll use an array index as the identifier; in a real scenario, the identifier would more likely be a key to locate the book information within a data store or service.

We'll call our new interface `OnSelectedBookChangeListener`. The interface looks like this:

```
public interface OnSelectedBookChangeListener {
  void onSelectedBookChanged(int bookIndex);
}
```

Making the fragment self-contained

The `BookListFragment` class needs to hide the details of user selections and instead translate each selection to a book identifier, which in our case is an array index. We first need to update the `BookListFragment` class to handle the radio button selections by implementing the `RadioGroup.OnCheckedChangeListener` interface as follows:

```
public class BookListFragment extends Fragment
    implements RadioGroup.OnCheckedChangeListener {

  @Override
  public void onCheckedChanged(RadioGroup radioGroup, int id)   {

  }
```

```
// Other members elided for clarity

}
```

Within the BookListFragment class' onCreateView method, we set the radio group's click listener as the BookListFragment class as shown here:

```
public View onCreateView(LayoutInflater inflater,
    ViewGroup container, Bundle savedInstanceState) {
  View viewHierarchy = inflater.inflate(
      R.layout.fragment_book_list, container, false);

  // Connect the listener to the radio group
  RadioGroup group = (RadioGroup)
  viewHierarchy.findViewById(R.id.bookSelectGroup);
  group.setOnCheckedChangeListener(this);

  return viewHierarchy;
}
```

There are a number of ways to determine the book index corresponding to the selected radio button such as setting the tag value on each radio button or using a lookup table. For simplicity, we'll create a simple method containing a switch statement like the following code:

```
int translateIdToIndex(int id) {
  int index = -1;
  switch (id) {
    case R.id.dynamicUiBook:
      index = 0 ;
      break;
    case R.id.android4NewBook:
      index = 1 ;
      break;
    case R.id.androidSysDevBook:
      index = 2 ;
      break;
    case R.id.androidEngineBook:
      index = 3 ;
      break;
    case R.id.androidDbProgBook:
      index = 4 ;
      break;
  }

  return index;
}
```

Fragment notification

A fragment can always access the activity on which it is placed using the getActivity method. Within the BookListFragment class' onClick method, we can use the getActivity method to access the activity, cast it to the OnSelectedBookChangeListener interface, and then call the onSelectedBookChanged method and pass it the book index for the selected radio button as shown in the following code:

```
public void onCheckedChanged(RadioGroup radioGroup, int id) {
    // Translate radio button to book index
    int bookIndex = translateIdToIndex(id);

    // Get parent Activity and send notification
    OnSelectedBookChangeListener listener =
        (OnSelectedBookChangeListener) getActivity();
    listener.onSelectedBookChanged(bookIndex);
}
```

The BookListFragment class now completely handles notifying the parent activity of each change in the user book selection.

Encapsulating fragment operations

Within the BookDescFragment class, we want to encapsulate any details about how the user interface is updated. We'll do this by providing a simple method that accepts the book index and handles the details of locating and displaying the book description. Before we can implement that method, we first need to update the BookDescFragment class' onCreateView method to retrieve the list of book descriptions, retrieve a reference to TextView identified by R.id.bookDescription, and assign both to class-level fields as shown here:

```
public class BookDescFragment extends Fragment {

    String[] mBookDescriptions;
    TextView mBookDescriptionTextView;

    @Override
    public View onCreateView(LayoutInflater inflater,
      ViewGroup container, Bundle savedInstanceState) {
      View viewHierarchy = inflater.inflate(
          R.layout.fragment_book_desc, container, false);

      // Load array of book descriptions
      mBookDescriptions = getResources().
```

```
        getStringArray(R.array.bookDescriptions);
    // Get reference to book description text view
    mBookDescriptionTextView = (TextView)
        viewHierarchy.findViewById(R.id.bookDescription);

    return viewHierarchy;
  }
}
```

We can now add a `setBook` method that accepts the book index, accesses the appropriate book description, and updates `mBookDescriptionTextView`. The `setBook` method appears as follows:

```
public void setBook(int bookIndex) {
    // Lookup the book description
    String bookDescription = mBookDescriptions[bookIndex];

    // Display it
    mBookDescriptionTextView.setText(bookDescription);
}
```

Loosely connecting the pieces

Good use of interfaces and encapsulation greatly simplify using any component, and fragments are no different. With the work we've done on the `BookListFragment` and `BookDescFragment` classes, our activity can now coordinate user interaction in `BookListFragment` by updating `BookDescFragment` in three simple steps:

1. Implement the `OnSelectedBookChangeListener` interface.
2. Get a reference to the `BookDescFragment` class.
3. Call the `BookDescFragment` class' `setBook` method.

Have a look at step 2 first. Unlike when working with views, an activity cannot directly reference the fragments contained within it. Instead, fragment handling is delegated to the `FragmentManager` class.

Each activity has a unique instance of the `FragmentManager` class. The `FragmentManager` class handles access to and management of all fragments within that activity. An activity accesses its `FragmentManager` instance with the `getFragmentManager` method.

When working with the Android Support Library, use the FragmentActivity class' getSupportFragmentManager method in place of the standard Activity class' getFragmentManager method to access the current FragmentManager instance.

With FragmentManager, an activity can access the contained fragments by calling the FragmentManager.findFragmentById method and passing the desired fragment's ID value from the layout resource.

FragmentManager is an important class with a number of powerful capabilities. We'll talk much more about FragmentManager in *Chapter 4, Working with Fragment Transactions*.

By using FragmentManager to access BookDescFragment, we can now implement the BookListFragment.OnSelectedBookChangeListener interface on our activity to update the displayed description for each user selection in BookListFragment.

```
public class MainActivity extends Activity
    implements OnSelectedBookChangeListener{

  @Override
  public void onSelectedBookChanged(int bookIndex) {
    // Access the FragmentManager
    FragmentManager fragmentManager = getFragmentManager();
    // Get the book description fragment
    BookDescFragment bookDescFragment = (BookDescFragment)
        fragmentManager.findFragmentById
          (R.id.fragmentDescription);
    // Display the book title
    if(bookDescFragment != null)
      bookDescFragment.setBook(bookIndex);
  }

  // other members elided for clarity
}
```

Fragments protect against the unexpected

The true test of user interface flexibility is in how well the user interface design and implementation hold up when encountering an unexpected change request. A well-designed fragment-based user interface allows us to create incredible dynamic user interfaces that can evolve and change with minimal impact on the code. As an example, let's make what could potentially be a major design change on our application.

Currently, the application always shows the book list and description on the same activity. The only difference is whether the fragments are positioned vertically or horizontally relative to one another. Imagine we receive feedback from our users that they don't like the way the app appears when viewed on a portrait-oriented handset. When viewed on a portrait-oriented handset, they would like the list and description to appear on separate activities. In all other cases, they want the app to continue to show the list and description side-by-side.

Evolving layout resource files

We first create a duplicate copy of the `activity_main.xml` resource file in the `layout` resource folder named `activity_book_desc.xml`. To do this in Android Studio, perform the following steps:

1. Right-click on the `activity_main.xml` file in the project explorer window and select **Copy**.

2. Right-click on the `layout` folder and select **Paste**.

3. Change the filename to `activity_book_desc.xml`.

Remove the fragment element for `BookListFragment` from the `activity_book_desc.xml` file so it now shows only `BookDescFragment` as in the following code:

```
<LinearLayout
    xmlns:tools=""http://schemas.android.com/tools""
    android:orientation=""vertical""
    android:layout_width=""match_parent""
    android:layout_height=""match_parent""
    xmlns:android=""http://schemas.android.com/apk/res/android"">

    <!-- Description of selected book  -->
    <fragment
        android:layout_width=""match_parent""
        android:layout_height=""0dp""
        android:layout_weight=""1""
        android:name=""com.jwhh.fragments_after.BookDescFragment""
```

```
        android:id=""@+id/fragmentDescription""
        tools:layout=""@layout/fragment_book_desc""/>

    </LinearLayout>
```

In the `activity_main.xml` resource file, remove `BookDescFragment` so that it now appears as follows:

```
    <LinearLayout
        xmlns:tools=""http://schemas.android.com/tools""
        android:orientation=""vertical""
        android:layout_width=""match_parent""
        android:layout_height=""match_parent""
        xmlns:android=""http://schemas.android.com/apk/res/android"">

    <!--    List of Book Titles   -->
    <fragment
        android:layout_width=""match_parent""
        android:layout_height=""0dp""
        android:layout_weight=""1""
        android:name=""com.jwhh.fragments_after.BookListFragment""
        android:id=""@+id/fragmentTitles""
        tools:layout=""@layout/fragment_book_list""/>

    </LinearLayout>
```

We now have layout resources for each of the activities. Remember that these changes will not affect the appearance of the app in scenarios that use the `activity_main_wide.xml` resource file.

Creating the book description activity

To display the book description, we add a simple activity named `BookDescActivity` that uses the `activity_book_desc.xml` layout resource. The activity relies on an "Intent extra" to pass the book index. Since `BookDescFragment` contains all the logic necessary to display a book description, we can simply get a reference to `BookDescFragment` and set the book index just as we did in the `MainActivity` class as shown here:

```
    public class BookDescActivity extends Activity {
      @Override
      protected void onCreate(Bundle savedInstanceState) {
        super.onCreate(savedInstanceState);
        setContentView(R.layout.activity_book_desc);
```

```
    // Retrieve the book index from the Activity Intent
    Intent intent = getIntent();
    int bookIndex = intent.getIntExtra(""bookIndex"", -1);

    if (bookIndex != -1) {
      // Use FragmentManager to access BookDescFragment
      FragmentManager fm = getFragmentManager();
      BookDescFragment bookDescFragment = (BookDescFragment)
          fm.findFragmentById(R.id.fragmentDescription);
      // Display the book title
      bookDescFragment.setBook(bookIndex);
    }
  }
}
```

Making the MainActivity class adaptive

The MainActivity class has some extra work to do now because the specific
fragments contained within it will vary. When running on a device with a screen
that is at least 600 dp wide or when running on a device in the large screen group,
the MainActivity class always contains an instance of BookDescFragment. On the
other hand, when running on other devices, the presence of BookDescFragment
will depend upon the device's current orientation. We could add code to the
MainActivity class to test for all of these various scenarios or we could take a
simpler approach, that is, check whether the activity contains an instance of the
BookDescFragment class.

Using this approach, we have the MainActivity class' onSelectedBookChanged
method to check the validity of BookDescFragment returned by FragmentManager.
If FragmentManager returns a valid reference, the method can call setBook on
BookDescFragment just as it has been. If the returned reference is not valid,
the onSelectedBookChanged method calls startActivity with an Intent
instance containing the information to display BookDescActivity that includes
bookIndex as an extra as shown in the following code:

```
public void onSelectedBookChanged(int bookIndex) {
  // Access the FragmentManager
  FragmentManager fm = getFragmentManager();
  // Get the book description fragment
  BookDescFragment bookDescFragment = (BookDescFragment)
      fm.findFragmentById(R.id.fragmentDescription);

  // Check validity of fragment reference
  if(bookDescFragment == null || !bookDescFragment.isVisible()){
```

```
    // Use activity to display description
    Intent intent = new Intent(this, BookDescActivity.class);
    intent.putExtra(""bookIndex"", bookIndex);
    startActivity(intent);
  }
  else {
    // Use contained fragment to display description
    bookDescFragment.setBook(bookIndex);
  }
}
```

Notice the `if` statement that checks the validity of `bookDescFragment`. In most cases, a simple check for whether the reference is null is all we need. The one exception is the case of when the app is run on a handset device on which the user has viewed the app in landscape orientation and then rotated the device to portrait. In this situation, the `BookDescFragment` instance is not visible but the activity's `FragmentManager` instance may be caching a reference to an invisible instance remaining from the landscape layout. For this reason, we check both for a null reference and for visibility. We'll discuss the details of fragment lifecycle, creation, and caching over the next two chapters.

We now have adaptability built into our app. The scenarios that use the `activity_main_wide.xml` resource file look as they always did. On portrait-oriented handset devices, our app provides the user interface with two separate activities: one for the book list and one for the book description. The application now appears on portrait-oriented handset devices as shown here:

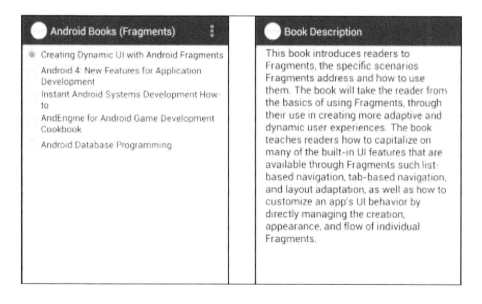

Summary

Fragments provide our applications with a level of user interface flexibility that would be difficult to achieve otherwise. By properly designing our application to use fragments and associating the fragment resources with the appropriate device characteristics, we're able to build apps that contain a rich user interface that automatically adapts to the wide variety of Android device form factors that exist. We get all of these capabilities while writing only minimal code.

In the next chapter, we dig into the lifecycle of fragments and explore how we can leverage the fragment lifecycle to create more responsive user interfaces and leverage specialized `Fragment` classes.

3
Fragment Lifecycle and Specialization

This chapter discusses the relationship of the lifecycle of fragments to that of activities, and demonstrates the appropriate programming actions at the various points in the lifecycle. The special purpose fragment classes `ListFragment` and `DialogFragment` are introduced with coverage of their use and how their behavior in the activity lifecycle differs from that of standard fragments.

The following topics are covered in this chapter:

- Fragment setup/display event sequence
- Fragment teardown/hide event sequence
- Working with the `ListFragment` class
- Working with the `DialogFragment` class
- Interacting with a `DialogFragment` class as a traditional `Dialog` class
- Wrapping an existing `Dialog` class in a `DialogFragment` class

By the end of this chapter, we will be able to coordinate the setup and teardown of fragments within their host activities, and be able to effectively utilize the `ListFragment` and `DialogFragment` classes.

Understanding the fragment lifecycle

One of the challenges of developing Android applications is assuring that our applications effectively handle the lifecycle of the application's activities. During the lifetime of an application, a given activity may be created, destroyed, and recreated many times. A simple action such as a user rotating a device from a portrait to landscape orientation, or vice-versa, normally causes the visible activity to be completely destroyed and recreated using the appropriate resources for the new orientation. Applications that do not cooperate effectively with this natural lifecycle will often crash or behave in some other undesirable manner.

As we know, each fragment instance exists within a single activity; therefore, that fragment must cooperate in some way with the activity lifecycle. In fact, not only do fragments cooperate with the activity lifecycle but also they are intimately connected.

In both the setup and display phase and hide and teardown phase, fragments provide many of the same lifecycle-related callback methods as activities. In addition, fragments provide additional lifecycle-related callback methods that relate to the fragment's relationship to the containing activity.

As our applications become more sophisticated and we work with more specialized implementations of the fragment class, understanding the fragment class' lifecycle and the relationship to the activity lifecycle is essential.

 If you are unfamiliar with the basics of Android's activity lifecycle callback methods, please see the *Activity Lifecycle* section of the *Android Activity* documentation at http://developer.android.com/reference/android/app/Activity.html#ActivityLifecycle.

Understanding fragment setup and display

Fragment setup and display is a multiphase process involving the fragment's association with an activity, the fragments' creation, and the standard lifecycle events of moving the activity into the running state (also known as the resumed or active state). Understanding the behavior of the lifecycle events and the associated callback methods is essential for using fragments effectively. Once we have an understanding of the lifecycle events and the callback methods, we'll look at just how the event callback methods are used.

The following diagram shows the sequence of lifecycle-related callback method calls that occur on fragments and activities during setup and display:

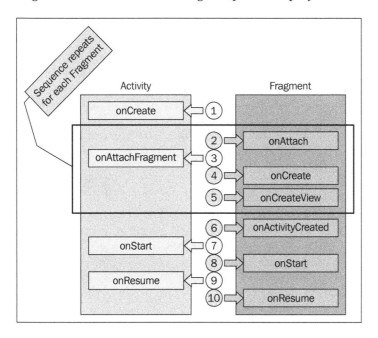

As you might expect, in most cases, the first step in the setup and display of a fragment occurs in the activity's onCreate method. In most cases, the activity calls the setContentView method from within the activity's onCreate callback method, which then loads the layout resource and triggers the activity's association with the contained fragments.

Notice what happens next. Before the fragment is ever created, the fragment is attached to the activity. The fragment is first notified of the attachment and receives a reference to the activity through the onAttach callback method. The activity is then notified and receives a reference to the fragment through the onAttachFragment callback method.

Although attaching the fragment to the activity prior to creating the fragment may seem unexpected, doing so is useful. In many cases, the fragment needs access to the activity during the creation process, because the activity often contains information that the fragment will display or that is otherwise important to the fragment creation process.

With the fragment attached to the activity, the fragment then performs general creation work in the `onCreate` method and then constructs the contained view hierarchy in the `onCreateView` method.

When an activity contains multiple fragments, Android calls the four methods: `Fragment.onAttach`, `Activity.onAttachFragment`, `Fragment.onCreate`, and `Fragment.onCreateView` in succession for one fragment before making any calls to these methods for the next fragment. This allows each fragment to complete the process of attachment and creation before the next fragment begins that process.

Once the sequence of calling these four methods completes for all the fragments, the remaining setup and display callback methods are called individually in succession for each fragment.

After the activity completes execution of its `onCreate` method, Android then calls each fragment's `onActivityCreated` method. The `onActivityCreated` method indicates that all views and fragments created by the activity's layout resource are now fully constructed and can be safely accessed.

At this point, the fragment receives the standard lifecycle callbacks on the `onStart` and `onResume` methods, just after the activity methods of the same name are each called. Any work performed in the fragment's `onStart` and `onResume` methods is very much like the work performed in the corresponding methods within an activity.

For many fragments, the only methods in this part of their lifecycle that are overridden are the `onCreate` and `onCreateView` methods, as we saw in the examples in the previous chapters.

Avoiding method name confusion

The activity and fragment classes have a number of commonly named callback methods, and most of these commonly named methods have a common purpose. One important exception is the `onCreateView` method. The purpose of this method is very different for each class.

As mentioned previously, Android calls the `Fragment` class' `onCreateView` method to give the fragment an opportunity to create and return the fragment's contained view hierarchy. This method is commonly overridden within a fragment.

The method of the same name in the `Activity` class is called repeatedly by the `LayoutInflater` class during the process of inflating a layout resource. Most activity implementations do not override this method.

Understanding fragment hide and teardown

Just as fragments behave in a similar way to activities during setup and display, they also behave in a similar way during hide and teardown, as shown in the following diagram:

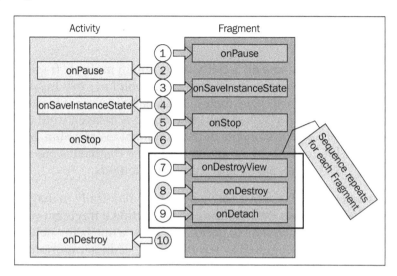

Initially during hide and teardown, fragments behave just as activities. When the user switches to another activity, each fragment's onPause, onSaveInstanceState, and onStop methods are called. For each method, the fragment implementation is called first, followed by the activity implementation.

After the onStop method is called, fragments begin to behave a little differently than activities. Consistent with the separation of fragment creation from fragment view hierarchy creation, fragment view hierarchy destruction is separate from fragment destruction. Following the call to the activity's onStop method, the fragment's onDestroyView method is called indicating that the view hierarchy returned by the fragment's onCreateView method is being destroyed. The fragment's onDestroy method is then called followed by the fragment's onDetach method. At this point, the fragment has no association with an activity and any calls to the getActivity method will return null.

For activities containing multiple fragments, Android calls the sequence of the three methods, onDestroyView, onDestroy, and onDetach, for an individual fragment, before beginning the sequence of calling these three methods for the next fragment. This groups the process of destroying and detaching each fragment similar to the way Android groups the process of attaching and creating each fragment. Once this sequence completes for all fragments, Android then calls the activity's onDestroy method.

Maximizing available resources

For the most part, lifecycle management for a fragment is very much like that of an activity. There is, however, one important exception: the two-phase nature of fragment creation and destruction. Fragments separate the creation and destruction of the fragment from the fragment's contained view hierarchy. This is because fragments have the ability to exist and be associated with an activity in the absence of the fragment's view hierarchy.

There are many scenarios where an activity may contain multiple fragments, but have only a subset of those fragments visible at any point in time. In such a case, the contained fragments can all have their onAttach and onCreate methods called. But the call to each fragment's onCreateView method is delayed until the time comes for the app to make the contents of that fragment visible. Similarly, when the time comes to hide the contents of a fragment, only the fragment's onDestroyView method is called, not the onDestroy and onDetach methods.

This behavior comes into play when fragments are dynamically managed within an activity. This behavior allows the overhead of associating a fragment with an activity and initializing the fragment's state to occur only once while being able to easily change the visibility of the fragment's view hierarchy. This is important when we explicitly manage the visibility of fragments using the FragmentTransaction class, and in certain action bar features that manage fragments. We'll talk about these issues in the next two chapters.

Managing a fragment state

For many fragment implementations, the most important callback method in the lifecycle sequence is the onSaveInstanceState method. Just as with an activity, this callback method provides the fragment with an opportunity to persist any state before the fragment is destroyed, such as when the user moves to another activity or when the user rotates the device to a different orientation. In both of these cases, the activity and contained fragments may be completely torn down and recreated. By persisting the fragment state in the onSaveInstanceState method, that state is latter passed back to the fragment in both the onCreate and onCreateView methods.

When managing the state of a fragment, you want to be sure to separate work that is general to the fragment's overall existence from work specific to setting up the view hierarchy. Any expensive initialization work that's general to the fragment's existence such as connecting to a data source, complex calculations, or resource allocations should occur in the onCreate method rather than the onCreateView method. This way, if only the fragment's view hierarchy is destroyed and the fragment remains intact, you avoid unnecessarily repeating expensive initialization work.

Special purpose fragment classes

Now that we understand the lifecycle of fragments, we can look at some of the specialized versions of the Fragment class. As we go through each of these specialized classes, remember they all ultimately inherit from the Fragment class and therefore experience the same lifecycle behavior. Many of these specialized classes have an impact on what operations are safe to perform at the various points in the lifecycle, and some of these classes even add their own lifecycle methods. Understanding each of these classes and their interaction with the fragment lifecycle is essential for using the classes effectively.

ListFragment

One of the simplest fragment-derived classes to use and yet one of the most helpful is the ListFragment class. The ListFragment class provides a fragment that encapsulates a ListView and, as the name implies, is useful for displaying lists of data.

Associating data with the list

Unlike the base Fragment class, we're not required to override the onCreateView callback method for the ListFragment class. The ListFragment class provides a standard appearance and only requires that we associate some data. The ListFragment class does all the work of creating the view hierarchy and displaying that data.

We associate data with the ListFragment class by calling the ListFragment class' setListAdapter method and passing a reference to an object that implements the ListAdapter interface. Android provides a number of classes that implement this interface such as ArrayAdapter, SimpleAdapter, and SimpleCursorAdapter. The specific class you use will depend on how your source data is stored. If none of the standard Android classes meet your specific requirements, you can create a custom implementation reasonably easy.

 For a discussion about creating a custom list adapter, see the Android tutorial *Displaying the Quick Contact Badge* at http://developer.android.com/training/contacts-provider/display-contact-badge.html.

The call to setListAdapter requires that the view hierarchy for the ListFragment be completely constructed. As a result, we normally do not call the setListAdapter method any earlier than the onActivityCreated callback method.

The `ListFragment` class wraps an instance of the `ListView` class, which is accessible through the `getListView` method. In most scenarios, we can feel free to interact with the contained `ListView` instance directly and take advantage of any features offered by the `ListView` class. The one very important exception is when we set the `ListAdapter` instance. Both the `ListFragment` and `ListView` classes expose a `setListAdapter` method, but we must be sure to use the `ListFragment` version of the method.

The `ListFragment` class relies on certain initialization behaviors that occur within the `ListFragment.setListAdapter` method; therefore, the process of calling the `setListAdapter` method directly on the contained `ListView` instance bypasses this initialization behavior and may cause the application to become unstable.

Separating data from display

Up until now, our application has used a fixed layout of several `RadioButton` views to display the list of books. Using a fixed layout to display such options is not generally a good choice, because any changes to the book list require that we go in and directly modify the fragment layout. In practice, we would prefer to have a layout that is independent of the specific titles. We could write code to dynamically generate the `RadioButton` views, but there is an easier way. We can instead use the `ListFragment` class.

By switching our application to use the `ListFragment` class, we can simply store the list of book titles in an array resource and associate the contents of that array resource with the `ListFragment` instance. In the event of adding more titles or needing to change one of the titles, we simply modify the array resource file. There is no need for us to make any changes to the actual fragment layout.

Our application already has all the book titles stored as individual string resources, so we just need to add an array resource for them. We'll add the book titles array to the `arrays.xml` resource file within the `values` resource folder where we currently have an array resource defined to hold the list of book descriptions.

Within the `resources` root element of the `arrays.xml` resource file, add a `string-array` element that includes a `name` attribute with a value of `bookTitles`. Within the `string-array` element, add an `item` for each book title that references the string resource for each title. We want to be sure that we list the book title array entries in the same order as the `bookDescription` array entries because we use the array index as the ID value for each book when we notify the activity of the user's book selection. The array resource entries for the book title and description arrays appear as follows:

```
<resources>
  <!-- Book Titles -->
```

```xml
<string-array name="bookTitles">
  <item>@string/dynamicUiTitle</item>
  <item>@string/android4NewTitle</item>
  <item>@string/androidSysDevTitle</item>
  <item>@string/androidEngineTitle</item>
  <item>@string/androidDbProgTitle</item>
</string-array>

<!-- Book Descriptions -->
<string-array name="bookDescriptions">
  <item>@string/dynamicUiDescription</item>
  <item>@string/android4NewDescription</item>
  <item>@string/androidSysDevDescription</item>
  <item>@string/androidEngineDescription</item>
  <item>@string/androidDbProgDescription</item>
</string-array>
</resources>
```

With the titles stored as an array resource, we can now easily create a `ListFragment` derived class to display the book titles.

Creating the ListFragment derived class

The first step is to add a new class to our project. To do this, we'll create a new class named `BookListFragment2` that extends the `ListFragment` class as shown in the following code line:

```java
class BookListFragment2 extends ListFragment {  }
```

Next, we override the `onActivityCreated` method as follows:

```java
public void onActivityCreated(Bundle savedInstanceState) {
  super.onActivityCreated(savedInstanceState);

  String[] bookTitles =
      getResources().getStringArray(R.array.bookTitles);
  ArrayAdapter<String> bookTitlesAdapter =
      new ArrayAdapter<String>(getActivity(),
      android.R.layout.simple_list_item_1, bookTitles);

  setListAdapter(bookTitlesAdapter);
}
```

In the `onActivityCreated` method, we first call the base class implementation that is required by all classes that extend `ListFragment`. We then load the `bookTitles` array resource and associate it with an instance of the `ArrayAdapter` class named `bookTitlesAdapter`. The array adapter takes the context as the first parameter, which we get by accessing the activity, and takes the array as the third parameter. The second parameter is the ID of the resource to use to lay out each entry in the list. This resource can be a custom resource or one of the built-in Android resources. In our case, we're using the built-in Android layout resource `android.R.layout. simple_list_item_1`, which displays a single string value for each row within the `ListView`. The last step is to call the `setListAdapter` method and pass the `bookTitlesAdapter` method.

 Creating a custom layout resource for the `ListFragment` class is just like doing so for the `ListView` class, and is discussed in detail in the Android developer documentation: `http://developer.android. com/reference/android/app/ListFragment.html`.

Handling ListFragment item selection

For our application to work correctly, we need to inform the activity each time the user selects one of the titles. Because we use an interface to loosely couple our fragment with the activity, this turns out to be a pretty simple task.

We first override the `ListFragment` class' `onListItemClick` method. The `ListFragment` class calls the `onListItemClick` method when the user selects an entry within the `ListFragment` instance. The `onListItemClick` method receives several selection-related parameters including the zero-based position of the selection. Our `ListFragment` is loaded from an array, so this position value corresponds to the selected title's array index.

With the `position` parameter value corresponding directly to the array index, all we have to do to inform the activity of the user selection is get a reference to the activity, cast it to our `OnSelectionChangeListener` interface, and call the interface's `onSelectedBookChanged` method, passing the `position` parameter value as shown in this code:

```
public void onListItemClick(ListView l, View v,
    int position, long id) {
  // Access the Activity and cast to the inteface
  OnSelectedBookChangeListener listener =
    (OnSelectedBookChangeListener)
```

```
        getActivity();

    // Notify the Activity of the selection
    listener.onSelectedBookChanged(position);
}
```

All the activity classes in our application that will use our `BookListFragment2` class already implement the `OnSelectionChangeListener` interface, so there is no change required to the activity classes.

Updating the layout resources

We now update the `activity_main.xml` resource file to use the `BookListFragment2` class instead of the original `BookListFragment` class as shown in the following code:

```
<LinearLayout
    android:orientation="vertical"
    android:layout_width="match_parent"
    android:layout_height="match_parent"
    xmlns:android="http://schemas.android.com/apk/res/android">

    <!-- List of Book Titles ** using the ListFragment **-->
    <fragment
        android:layout_width="match_parent"
        android:layout_height="0dp"
        android:layout_weight="1"
        android:name="com.jwhh.fragments.BookListFragment2"
        android:id="@+id/fragmentTitles"/>

    <!-- Description of selected book -->
    <fragment
        android:layout_width="match_parent"
        android:layout_height="0dp"
        android:layout_weight="1"
        android:name="com.jwhh.fragments.BookDescFragment"
        android:id="@+id/fragmentDescription"/>
</LinearLayout>
```

We need to make the same change in the `activity_main_wide.xml` file.

Our program is now fully functional using the `ListFragment` class and appears as follows:

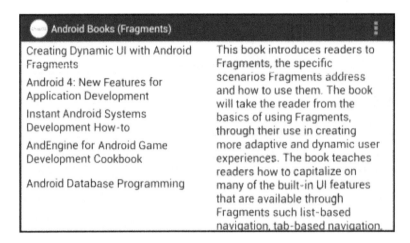

Any changes that we need to make to the titles can now all be made in the resources file and require no changes to the user interface code.

DialogFragment

Up until now we've been looking at fragments as a new way to divide our application's user interface into subsections of the available display area. Although fragments are new, the concept of having an aspect of our application user interface as a subsection of the available display area is not new. Any time an application displays a dialog, the application is doing exactly that.

Historically, the challenge of working with dialogs is that even though they are conceptually just another window within an application, we must handle many of the tasks related to dialogs differently than other aspects of our application user interface. Doing something as simple as handling a button click requires a dialog-specific interface, `DialogInterface.OnClickListener`, rather than the `View.OnClickListener` interface that we use when handling a `click` event from non-dialog related parts of our user interface code. An even more complicated issue is that of orientation changes. Dialogs automatically close in response to an orientation change and therefore can create inconsistent application behavior if a user changes device orientation while a dialog is visible.

The `DialogFragment` class eliminates much of the special handling related to dialogs. With the `DialogFragment` class, displaying and managing a dialog becomes much more consistent with other aspects of our application user interface.

Styles

When an application displays an instance of the DialogFragment class, the window for the DialogFragment instance has up to three parts to it: layout area, title, and frame. A DialogFragment instance always contains the layout area, but we can control whether it includes the title and frame by setting the DialogFragment class' style using the setStyle method. The DialogFragment class supports four styles with an instance of the DialogFragment class having exactly one style applied. The following table shows the four available styles:

Style	Has Title	Has Frame	Accepts Input
STYLE_NORMAL	Yes	Yes	Yes
STYLE_NO_TITLE	No	Yes	Yes
STYLE_NO_FRAME	No	No	Yes
STYLE_NO_INPUT	No	No	No

Notice that the styles remove features cumulatively. For example, STYLE_NO_TITLE indicates no title whereas STYLE_NO_FRAME indicates no frame and no title. If we do not call the setStyle method, Android creates the DialogFragment instance with the style set to STYLE_NORMAL.

The style affects the remainder of the behavior of the DialogFragment class and therefore must be set in the onCreate callback method. An attempt to set the DialogFragment class' style any later in the lifecycle is ignored.

If you wish to provide the dialog with a special theme, the theme's resource ID can also be passed to the setStyle method. To allow Android to select an appropriate theme based on the style, simply pass 0 as the theme resource ID. The following code sets the DialogFragment instance to have no title and use the Android-selected theme for that style:

```
class MyDialogFragment extends DialogFragment {
  public void onCreate(Bundle savedInstanceState) {
    super.onCreate(savedInstanceState);

    setStyle(DialogFragment.STYLE_NO_TITLE, 0);
  }
}
```

Layout

Populating the layout of an instance of the `DialogFragment` class is just like that of a standard fragment derived class. We simply override the `onCreateView` method and inflate the layout resource.

```
public View onCreateView(LayoutInflater inflater,
    ViewGroup container, Bundle savedInstanceState) {
  View theView = inflater.inflate(R.layout.fragment_my_dialog,
      container, false);
  return theView;
}
```

Creating a layout resource for use with a `DialogFragment` derived class works exactly as creating a layout resource for any other fragment derived class. To have our `DialogFragment` instance display a line of text and two buttons, we define the `fragment_my_dialog.xml` layout resource as shown in the following XML:

```xml
<LinearLayout
    xmlns:android="http://schemas.android.com/apk/res/android"
    android:orientation="vertical"
    android:layout_width="match_parent"
    android:layout_height="match_parent">

  <!-- Text -->
  <TextView
      android:layout_width="fill_parent"
      android:layout_height="0px"
      android:layout_weight="1"
      android:text="@string/dialogSimpleFragmentPrompt"
      android:layout_margin="16dp"/>

  <!-- Two buttons side-by-side -->
  <LinearLayout
      android:layout_width="fill_parent"
      android:layout_height="0px"
      android:orientation="horizontal"
      android:layout_weight="3">
    <Button
        android:id="@+id/btnYes"
        android:layout_width="0px"
        android:layout_height="wrap_content"
```

```
            android:layout_weight="1"
            android:text="@string/text_yes"
            android:layout_margin="16dp"/>
        <Button
            android:id="@+id/btnNo"
            android:layout_width="0px"
            android:layout_height="wrap_content"
            android:layout_weight="1"
            android:text="@string/text_no"
            android:layout_margin="16dp"/>
    </LinearLayout>
</LinearLayout>
```

DialogFragment display

Displaying our `DialogFragment` derived class is largely just a matter of creating the class instance and calling the `show` method. We need to keep in mind though that although our `DialogFragment` instance appears as a standard dialog when it displays, it is actually a fragment. Like all fragments, it is managed by the containing activity's `FragmentManager` instance. As a result, we need to pass a reference to the activity's `FragmentManager` instance as part of the call to the `DialogFragment` class `show` method as we do in the following code:

```
MyDialogFragment theDialog = new MyDialogFragment();
theDialog.show(getFragmentManager(), null);
```

With our `DialogFragment` derived class' style set to `STYLE_NO_TITLE` and using the `fragment_my_dialog.xml` layout resource file shown earlier, the previous code displays the following:

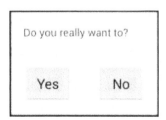

Event handling

One of the key values of the `DialogFragment` class is that it provides greater consistency in our code than is available when using the traditional `Dialog` class. Most aspects of working with the `DialogFragment` class are the same as when working with other fragments. No longer does displaying a dialog have to be handled so much differently than other aspects of our application user interface. For example, no special handling is required to deal with orientation changes. Another place where this greater consistency is evident is in event handling, because our button click event handling can use the standard view class event interfaces.

To handle the button clicks, our `DialogFragment` derived class simply implements the `View.OnClickListener` interface. The following code shows setting the yes and no button click events to call back to our `DialogFragment` derived class in our class' `onCreateView` callback method:

```
public View onCreateView(LayoutInflater inflater,
    ViewGroup container, Bundle savedInstanceState) {
  View theView = inflater.inflate(
      R.layout.fragment_my_dialog, container, false);

  // Connect the Yes button click event and request focus
  View yesButton = theView.findViewById(R.id.btnYes);
  yesButton.setOnClickListener(this);
  yesButton.requestFocus();

  // Connect the No button click event
  View noButton = theView.findViewById(R.id.btnNo);
  noButton.setOnClickListener(this);

  return theView;
}
```

Notice that we're setting up the button click handling just as we would if we were working within any other fragment or even directly within the activity.

We can also handle notifying the activity of the user's interaction with the `DialogFragment` derived class consistently with the way we do with other fragments. Just as we did in the previous chapter, our `DialogFragment` derived class simply provides an interface for notifying the activity which of the available buttons the user selects, as shown in the following code:

```
public class MyDialogFragment extends DialogFragment
    implements View.OnClickListener {

  // Interface Activity implements for notification
```

```
public interface OnButtonClickListener {
  void onButtonClick(int buttonId);
}
// Other members elided for clarity
}
```

As long as the activity implements the interface, our `DialogFragment` derived class can notify the activity of which button the user clicked.

In the handler for our button click events, we'll follow the same pattern we did in the previous chapter. We access the containing activity, cast it to the expected interface, and call the interface method, as shown in the following code:

```
public void onClick(View view) {
  int buttonId = view.getId();

  // Notify the Activity of the button selection
  OnButtonClickListener parentActivity =
      (OnButtonClickListener) getActivity();
  parentActivity.onButtonClick(buttonId);

  // Close the dialog fragment
  dismiss();
}
```

Notice that there is one bit of special handling in the previous method. Just as with the traditional `Dialog` class, we must call the `dismiss` method on the `DialogFragment` derived class when we no longer wish to display it.

Dialog identity

Although we treat our `DialogFragment` derived class as just another fragment, it still has a part of its identity that is tied to the traditional `Dialog` class. In fact, Android actually wraps our `DialogFragment` derived class within a traditional `Dialog` instance. This occurs in a callback method, specific to the `DialogFragment` class, named `onCreateDialog` that Android calls just prior to calling the `onCreateView` callback method.

The `Dialog` instance that the `onCreateDialog` method returns is the window that is ultimately displayed to the user. The layout we create within our `DialogFragment` derived class is simply wrapped within the `Dialog` window. We can access that `Dialog` instance later in the lifecycle to access `Dialog` related behavior or even override the method to provide our own `Dialog` instance.

Accessing Dialog related behavior

Accessing the Dialog related behavior of our DialogFragment derived class requires a reference to the Dialog instance created in the onCreateDialog method. We retrieve that reference by calling the getDialog method. Once we have the reference to the Dialog instance, we can access aspects of the class' dialog identity that are not otherwise available.

When we create a DialogFragment derived class with the style set to STYLE_NORMAL, the displayed dialog includes a title area above the layout area. The value of the title can only be set by calling the setTitle method on the Dialog instance that wraps our DialogFragment instance. A similar issue comes up in dealing with the dialog cancellation behavior. By default, the user can cancel a dialog by tapping on the activity behind the dialog. In many cases, this may be unacceptable as we want to require the user to acknowledge one of the choices within the dialog. The following code sets these Dialog related behaviors after the button click handling is set up:

```
public View onCreateView(LayoutInflater inflater,
    ViewGroup container, Bundle savedInstanceState) {
  View theView = inflater.inflate(R.layout.fragment_my_dialog,
      container, false);

  View yesButton = theView.findViewById(R.id.btnYes);
  yesButton.setOnClickListener(this);
  yesButton.requestFocus();

  View noButton = theView.findViewById(R.id.btnNo);
  noButton.setOnClickListener(this);

  // Set the dialog aspects of the dialog fragment
  Dialog dialog = getDialog();
  dialog.setTitle(getString(R.string.myDialogFragmentTitle));
  dialog.setCanceledOnTouchOutside(false);

  return theView;
}
```

The code first sets the dialog title and then sets the option to prevent the user from closing the dialog by tapping on the activity window. For the call to the setTitle method to work, we will need to change the call to the setStyle method in the onCreate callback method to set the style to STYLE_NORMAL so that the dialog will have a title area.

Wrapping an existing dialog in a fragment

There may be times where we like the programming consistency that the
DialogFragment class offers, but want to take advantage of the features
provided by a class that derives from the traditional Dialog class. By overriding
the DialogFragment class' onCreateDialog method, we can do exactly that.
Overriding the onCreateDialog method allows us to replace the DialogFragment
class' default Dialog instance with one we create. A great example of when this
is useful is in leveraging the Android AlertDialog class.

The AlertDialog class provides a variety of default behaviors and allows us to
display text, an icon, and buttons all without having to create a layout resource.
There is something we must keep in mind when we're leveraging a class that
inherits from the traditional Dialog class. Although outside interaction with our
class will be consistent with other DialogFragment derived classes, any interactions
with the traditional Dialog class that occur within our DialogFragment derived
class will be done in the traditional Dialog class way. For example, to create a
DialogFragment derived class that utilizes the AlertDialog class requires that our
class implements the Dialog class way of handling click events that is to implement
the DialogInterface.OnClickListener interface as shown in the following code:

```
public class AlertDialogFragment extends DialogFragment
    implements DialogInterface.OnClickListener{   }
```

Within our class' onCreateDialog method, we create the AlertDialog instance
using the AlertDialog.Builder class just as if we were going to display the
AlertDialog instance directly. Within the onCreateDialog method we set all the
options on the AlertDialog.Builder instance, including the title, message, icon,
and buttons. Notice, though, that we never call the AlertDialog.Builder class'
show method, but instead call its create method. We then take the reference to
the newly created AlertDialog instance and return it from the onCreateDialog
method. All of these steps are shown in the following code:

```
public Dialog onCreateDialog(Bundle savedInstanceState) {
  // Create the Builder for the AlertDialog
  AlertDialog.Builder builder =
      new AlertDialog.Builder(getActivity());

  // Set the AlertDialog options
  builder.setTitle(R.string.alert_dialog_title)
      .setMessage(R.string.alert_dialog_message)
      .setIcon(R.drawable.ic_launcher)
      .setCancelable(false)
      .setPositiveButton(R.string.text_yes, this)
```

```
                .setNegativeButton(R.string.text_no, this);

        // Create and return the AlertDialog
        AlertDialog alertDialog = builder.create();
        return alertDialog;
    }
```

The `Dialog` instance we create is now managed as a part of the `DialogFragment` instance. Everything else we do with our `AlertDialogFragment` class will be just as it is with the other `DialogFragment` derived classes we create.

When our app shows our `AlertDialogFragment` class, it appears as the following screenshot:

Notice that we didn't need to override the `onCreateView` callback method, because the `Dialog` instance we create in the `onCreateDialog` callback method provides the desired display characteristics.

Overriding the `DialogFragment` class' `onCreateDialog` callback method is a powerful technique that allows us to enjoy the benefits of the `DialogFragment` class while still leveraging existing investment we may have in traditional `Dialog` classes, whether they be a built-in class such as the `AlertDialog` class or some custom `Dialog` class we may have as part of our own code library.

Summary

Understanding the fragment lifecycle empowers us to leverage the phases of creation and destruction of fragments to more efficiently manage fragments and the data associated with them. By working with this natural lifecycle, we can take advantage of the specialized fragment classes to create a rich user experience, while following a more consistent programming model than was previously available.

In the next chapter, we build on our understanding of the fragment lifecycle to take more direct control of fragments to dynamically add and remove them within individual activities.

4
Working with Fragment Transactions

This chapter covers dynamically managing fragments within an activity, implementing back button behavior, and monitoring user interaction with the back button.

Let's have a look at the topics covered:

- Understanding `FragmentTransactions`
- Dynamically adding and removing fragments
- Managing fragment UI separate from activity relationship
- Adding back button support to `FragmentTransactions`

By the end of this chapter, we will be able to create interactive UIs that use fragments to dynamically change the appearance of the screen in response to user actions.

Intentional screen management

Until now, we've considered each activity to always correspond to a single screen in our application. We've used fragments only to represent subsections within each screen. As an example, let's think back to the way we've constructed our book-browsing application. In the case of a wide-display device, our application uses a single activity containing two fragments. One fragment displays the list of book titles, and the other fragment displays the description of the currently selected book. Because both of these fragments appear on the screen at the same time, we display and manage them from a single activity. In the case of a portrait-oriented handset, we chose to display the book list and the book description on separate screens. Because the two fragments do not appear on the screen at the same time, we manage them in separate activities.

An interesting thing is that the tasks our application performs are identical in both cases. The only difference is how much information we're able to display on the screen at one time. That one detail causes us to add an extra activity to our application. We also increase the complexity of our application because the code to launch a new activity is more involved than the code we use to simply update a fragment within the same activity. And we have duplicated code in the activities because they both interact with the book description fragment.

As you'll recall, when we started talking about fragments in *Chapter 1, Fragments and UI Modularization*, we mentioned that one of the key values of fragments is that they help reduce unnecessary complications, activity proliferation, and logic duplication. Yet as the application is currently written, we're experiencing all of those things.

We need to evolve our thinking about UI design a little further. Rather than having activities within our application that simply react to what information happens to fit on the device's physical display, we instead need to focus on intentionally managing the relationship between the screens in our application and the corresponding activities.

To the user, the experience of moving to a new screen simply means that the view layout they are looking at is replaced with a different view layout. Historically, we've tended to design our applications so that each activity has a relatively fixed layout. As a result, moving the user to a new screen has required displaying a new activity, but fragments give us another option.

Rather than simply using fragments to manage logical subsections of the screen, we can also use them to manage logical groupings of an entire screen. We can then dynamically manage the fragments within an activity to change from one fragment to another. This gives the user the experience of moving from one screen to the next while giving us the convenience of managing common user interface elements within a single activity.

Dynamically managing fragments

The process of dynamically managing fragments commonly involves multiple steps. The steps may be simple like removing one fragment and adding another, or they may be more complex, involving the removal and addition of multiple fragments. In any case, we need to be certain that all dynamic changes to the fragments within an activity that constitute a shift from one application screen to the next occur together as a single unit of work. Android does this by grouping the steps into transactions using the `FragmentTransaction` class.

Conceptually, the FragmentTransaction class behaves in a manner consistent with other transaction models: start the transaction, identify the desired changes, and commit the transaction once all changes within that unit of work are identified.

When we're ready to make changes, we start a new FragmentTransaction instance by calling the beginTransaction method on the activity's FragmentManager instance, which returns back a reference to a FragmentTransaction instance. We then use the new FragmentTransaction instance to identify the desired changes to the list of displayed fragments within the activity. While we're in the transaction, these changes are queued up but not yet applied. Finally, when we've identified all the desired changes, we call the FragmentTransaction class' commit method.

Once all the changes in the transaction are applied, our application display is updated to reflect those changes, giving the user the feel of moving to a new screen of our application. Although a number of steps have occurred within our application, from the user's perspective everything behaves just as if we had displayed a new activity.

Deferred execution of transaction changes

The call to the commit method does not apply the changes immediately.

When we work with the FragmentTransaction class, we are not doing any direct work on the application user interface. Instead, we're building a To-Do list of work to be done to the user interface in the future. Each method that we call on a FragmentTransaction instance adds another To-Do item to the list. When we're done adding to the To-Do list and we call the commit method, those instructions get packaged up and sent to the main UI thread's message queue. The UI thread then walks through the list, performing the actual user interface work on behalf of the FragmentTransaction instance.

The deferred execution of the work performed within a FragmentTransaction instance works well in most cases. It can, however, create problems if our application code needs to find a fragment or interact with a view that is added by a fragment immediately following the call to the commit method. Although such a requirement is not normally the case, it does sometimes come up.

If we do have such a requirement, we can force the FragmentTransaction instance's work to be executed immediately by calling the FragmentManager class' executePendingTransactions method after the call to the FragmentTransaction instance's commit method. When a call to the executePendingTransactions method returns, we know that all the committed FragmentTransaction work has been performed.

We need to be careful by only calling the `executePendingTransactions` method on the main UI thread; this method causes the pending user interface work to execute, and therefore triggers direct interaction with the user interface.

Adding and removing fragments

There are a number of methods available on the `FragmentTransaction` class to manipulate the fragments within an activity, but the most fundamental are the `add` and `remove` methods.

The `add` method allows us to place a newly created fragment instance within a specific view group of our activity as shown here:

```
// Begin the transaction
FragmentManager fm = getFragmentManager();
FragmentTransaction ft = fm.beginTransaction();

// Create the Fragment and add
BookListFragment2 listFragment = new BookListFragment2();
ft.add(R.id.layoutRoot, listFragment, "bookList");

// Commit the changes
ft.commit();
```

We first create a new `FragmentTransaction` instance using the activity's `FragmentManager` instance. We then create a new instance of our `BookListFragment2` class and attach it to the activity as a child of the `LinearLayout` view group identified by the `R.id.layoutRoot` ID value. Finally, we commit the `FragmentTransaction` instance indicating that we're done making changes.

The string value, `"bookList"`, that we pass as the third parameter to the `add` method is simply a tag value. We can use the tag value to later locate the fragment instance in much the same way as we might use the ID value. When adding fragments dynamically, we use tags as identifiers rather than ID values simply because there is no way to associate an ID value with a dynamically added fragment.

The tag value comes in handy when we're ready to display a different fragment because we need to have a reference to the existing fragment to pass to the `remove` method so that we can remove it before adding a new fragment. The following code shows how we can update the display to show the `BookDescFragment` class in place of the `BookListFragment2` class we added in the previous code:

```
FragmentManager fm = getFragmentManager();
Fragment listFragment = fm.findFragmentByTag("bookList");
BookDescFragment bookDescFragment = new BookDescFragment();
FragmentTransaction ft = fm.beginTransaction();
ft.remove(listFragment);
ft.add(R.id.layoutRoot, bookDescFragment, "bookDescription");
ft.commit();
```

We begin by using the tag value to find our existing `BookListFragment2` instance using the `FragmentManager` class' `findFragmentByTag` method. We then create an instance of the new fragment we wish to add. Now that we have references to the fragment we want to remove and the one we want to add, we begin fragment transaction. Within the transaction, we remove the `BookListFragment2` instance by passing the reference to the `FragmentTransaction` class' `remove` method and then add the new fragment using the `add` method just as we did earlier. Finally, we call the `commit` method to allow the changes to be made.

This process of removing the fragment instance under a particular view group and adding another in its place occurs frequently enough that the `FragmentTransaction` class includes a convenient method named `replace`. The `replace` method allows us to simply identify the information for the fragment we wish to add. It takes care of the details of removing any other fragments that may exist within the target view group. Using the `replace` method, the code to remove the `BookListFragment2` instance and add the `BookDescFragment` instance can be written as follows:

```
FragmentManager fm = getFragmentManager();
bookDescFragment = new BookDescFragment();
FragmentTransaction ft = fm.beginTransaction();
ft.replace(R.id.layoutRoot, bookDescFragment, "bookDescription");
ft.commit();
```

Notice that this code, with the exception of the method name, is identical to the case of simply adding a fragment. We create our fragment instance, and then within the `FragmentTransaction` call, the `replace` method passes the ID of the target view group, fragment instance, and tag. The `replace` method handles the details of removing any fragment that may currently be within the `R.id.layoutRoot` view group. It then adds the `BookDescFragment` instance to the view group.

Supporting the back button

As we move to this model of managing our application screens as fragments, we need to be sure that we're providing the user with an experience consistent with their expectations. An area that requires special attention is our application's handling of the back button.

When a user interacts with the applications on their device, they naturally move forward through various application screens. The normal behavior is that a user can move back to a previous screen at any time by tapping the back button. This works because each time an application displays a new activity, Android automatically adds that activity to the Android back stack. This results in the expected behavior of the user moving to the previous activity with each tap of the back button.

This behavior is based on the assumption that one activity equals one application screen; an assumption that is no longer correct. When we transition the user from one application screen to another using the `FragmentTransaction` class, the application continues to display the same activity, leaving the back stack with no awareness of our application's new screen. This results in the application appearing to jump back multiple screens in response to the user tapping the back button because the back stack returns the user directly to the previous activity ignoring any intermediate changes made to the current activity.

The following figure demonstrates the issue:

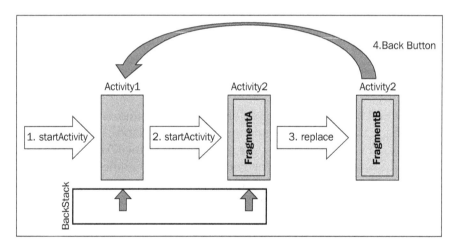

1. An application initially calls the startActivity method to display an instance of Activity1. Activity1 is automatically added to the back stack and is currently at the top of the stack.

2. Activity1 then calls the startActivity method to display Activity2, which uses the FragmentTransaction.add method to add FragmentA. Activity2 is automatically added to the top of the back stack.

3. Next, Activity2 uses the FragmentTransaction.replace method to display FragmentB in place of FragmentA. As far as the user is concerned, the application is displaying a new screen showing the contents of FragmentB. The problem is that the back stack is unchanged.

4. When the user now taps the back button, his/her expectation is that the app should display the previous screen, FragmentA, but instead when Android pops the back stack, the next screen it encounters is Activity1.

We resolve this issue by calling the FragmentTransaction class' addToBackStack method within the FragmentTransaction instance that displays FragmentB. The addToBackStack method adds the changes within the transaction to the top of the back stack. This allows the user to use the back button to move through the application screens created within the FragmentTransaction instance just as one does with screens created by showing an activity.

We can call the addToBackStack method at any point during the transaction prior to calling the commit method. The addToBackStack method optionally accepts a string parameter that can be used to name the location in the back stack. This is useful if you wish to programmatically manipulate the back stack later, but in most cases this parameter value can be passed as null. We'll see the addToBackStack method in action shortly as we modify our application to use a more adaptive layout.

Creating an adaptive application layout

Let's put our discussion of dynamic fragment management into practice by updating our application to work with just a single activity. This one activity will handle both scenarios: wide-display devices where both fragments appear side-by-side and portrait-oriented handsets where the fragments appear as two separate screens. As a reminder, the application appears as shown in the following screenshot in each scenario:

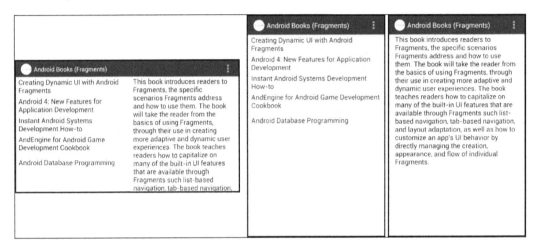

In our application, we'll leave the wide-display aspect of the program alone because static layout management is working fine there. Our work is on the portrait-oriented handset aspect of the application. For these devices, we'll update the application's main activity to dynamically switch between displaying the fragment containing the list of books and the fragment displaying the selected book description.

Updating the layout to support dynamic fragments

Before we write any code to dynamically manage the fragments within our application, we first need to modify the activity layout resource for portrait-oriented handset devices. That resource is contained in the `activity_main.xml` layout resource file and currently appears as shown here:

```
<LinearLayout
    xmlns:tools="http://schemas.android.com/tools"
    android:orientation="vertical"
    android:layout_width="match_parent"
```

```
        android:layout_height="match_parent"
        xmlns:android="http://schemas.android.com/apk/res/android">
    <!--    List of Book Titles    -->
    <fragment
        android:layout_width="match_parent"
        android:layout_height="0dp"
        android:layout_weight="1"
        android:name="com.jwhh.fragments.BookListFragment2"
        android:id="@+id/fragmentTitles"
        tools:layout="@layout/fragment_book_list"/>
</LinearLayout>
```

We need to make two changes to the layout resource. The first is to add an ID attribute to the `LinearLayout` view group so that we can easily locate it in code. The other change is to completely remove the `fragment` element. The updated layout resource now contains only the `LinearLayout` view group, which includes an ID attribute value of `@+id/layoutRoot`. The layout resource now appears as shown here:

```
<LinearLayout
    xmlns:tools="http://schemas.android.com/tools"
    android:id="@+id/layoutRoot"
    android:orientation="vertical"
    android:layout_width="match_parent"
    android:layout_height="match_parent"
    xmlns:android="http://schemas.android.com/apk/res/android">
</LinearLayout>
```

We still want our application to initially display the book list fragment, so removing the `fragment` element may seem like a strange change, but doing so is essential as we move our application to dynamically manage the fragments. We will eventually need to remove the book list fragment to replace it with the book description fragment. If we were to leave the book list fragment in the layout resource, our attempt to dynamically remove it later would silently fail.

 Only dynamically added fragments can be dynamically removed. Attempting to dynamically remove a fragment that was statically added with the `fragment` element in a layout resource will silently fail.

Adapting to device differences

When our application is running on a portrait-oriented handset device, the activity needs to programmatically load the fragment containing the book list. This is the same Fragment class, BookListFragment2, we were previously loading with the fragment element in the activity_main.xml layout resource file. Before we load the book list fragment, we first need to determine whether we're running on a device that requires dynamic fragment management. Remember that for the wide-display devices, we're going to leave the static fragment management in place.

There'll be a couple of places in our code where we'll need to take different logic paths depending on which layout we're using, so we'll need to add a boolean class-level field to the activity where we can store whether we're using dynamic or static fragment management.

```
boolean mIsDynamic;
```

We could interrogate the device for its specific characteristics such as screen size and orientation. But remember that much of our previous work was to configure our application to take advantage of the Android resource system to automatically load the appropriate layout resources based on the device characteristics. Rather than repeating those characteristics checks in code, we can instead simply include the code to determine which layout resource was loaded. The layout resource for wide-display devices we created earlier, activity_main_wide.xml, statically loads both the book list fragment and the book description fragment. We can include in our activity's onCreate method code to determine if the loaded layout resource includes one of those fragments as shown here:

```
public class MainActivity extends Activity
    implements BookListFragment.OnSelectedBookChangeListener {

  protected void onCreate(Bundle savedInstanceState) {
    super.onCreate(savedInstanceState);
    setContentView(R.layout.activity_main_dynamic);

    // Get the book description fragment
    FragmentManager fm = getFragmentManager();
    Fragment bookDescFragment =
        fm.findFragmentById(R.id.fragmentDescription);

    // If not found than we're doing dynamic mgmt
    mIsDynamic = bookDescFragment == null ||
        !bookDescFragment.isInLayout();
  }

  // Other members elided for clarity
}
```

When the call to the `setContentView` method returns, we know that the appropriate layout resource for the current device has been loaded. We then use the `FragmentManager` instance to search for the fragment with an ID value of `R.id.fragmentDescription` that is included in the layout resource for wide-display devices but not the layout resource for portrait-oriented handsets. A return value of `null` indicates that the fragment was not loaded and we are, therefore, on a device that requires us to dynamically manage the fragments. In addition to the test for null, we also include the call to the `isInLayout` method to protect against one special case scenario.

In the scenario where the device is in a landscape layout and then rotated to portrait, a cached instance to the fragment identified by `R.id.fragmentDescription` may still exist even though in the current orientation the activity is not using the fragment. By calling the `isInLayout` method, we're able to determine whether the returned reference is part of the currently loaded layout. With this, our test to set the `mIsDynamic` member variable effectively says that we'll set `mIsDynamic` to true when the `R.id.fragmentDescription` fragment is not found (equals `null`) or it's found but not part of the currently loaded layout (`!bookDescFragment.isInLayout`).

Dynamically loading a fragment at startup

Now that we're able to determine whether dynamically loading the book list fragment is necessary, we add the code to do so to our `onCreate` method as shown here:

```
protected void onCreate(Bundle savedInstanceState) {
    super.onCreate(savedInstanceState);
    setContentView(R.layout.activity_main_dynamic);

    // Get the book description fragment
    FragmentManager fm = getFragmentManager();
    Fragment bookDescFragment =
        fm.findFragmentById(R.id.fragmentDescription);

    // If not found than we're doing dynamic mgmt
    mIsDynamic = bookDescFragment == null ||
        !bookDescFragment.isInLayout();

    // Load the list fragment if necessary
    if (mIsDynamic) {
        // Begin transaction
        FragmentTransaction ft = fm.beginTransaction();

        // Create the Fragment and add
        BookListFragment2 listFragment = new BookListFragment2();
```

```
        ft.add(R.id.layoutRoot, listFragment, "bookList");

        // Commit the changes
        ft.commit();
      }
    }
```

Following the check to determine if we're on a device that requires dynamic fragment management, we include `FragmentTransaction` to add an instance of the `BookListFragment2` class to the activity as a child of the `LinearLayout` view group identified by the id value `R.id.layoutRoot`. This code capitalizes on the changes we made to the `activity_main.xml` resource file of removing the `fragment` element and including an ID value on the `LinearLayout` view group.

Now that we're dynamically loading the book list, we're ready to get rid of that other activity.

Transitioning between fragments

As you'll recall, whenever the user selects a book title within the `BookListFragment2` class, the fragment notifies the main activity by calling the `onSelectedBookChanged` method by passing the index of the selected book. The `onSelectedBookChanged` method currently appears as follows:

```
public void onSelectedBookChanged(int bookIndex) {
  FragmentManager fm = getFragmentManager();
  // Get the book description fragment
  BookDescFragment bookDescFragment = (BookDescFragment)
      fm.findFragmentById(R.id.fragmentDescription);

  // Check validity of fragment reference
  if(bookDescFragment == null || !bookDescFragment.isVisible()){
    // Use activity to display description
    Intent intent = new Intent(this, BookDescActivity.class);
    intent.putExtra("bookIndex", bookIndex);
    startActivity(intent);
  }
  else {
    // Use contained fragment to display description
    bookDescFragment.setBook(bookIndex);
  }
}
```

In the current implementation, we use a technique similar to what we did in the `onCreate` method to determine which layout is loaded; we try to find the book description fragment within the currently loaded layout. If we find it, we know the current layout includes the fragment and so we go ahead and set the book description directly on the fragment. If we don't find it, we call the `startActivity` method to display the activity that does contain the book description fragment.

In this scenario, handing off to the other activity isn't too bad because we only pass a simple integer value to the other activity. In practice though, the need to pass data over to another activity can be complicated. This is especially true if there are a large number of values or if some of those values are object types that cannot be directly passed in an `Intent` instance without additional coding. As we already have all the necessary handling to interact with the fragment in the current activity, we'd prefer to handle it consistently in all cases.

Eliminating redundant handling

To get started, we can strip any code in the current implementation that deals with starting an activity. We can also avoid repeating the check for the book description fragment because we performed that check earlier in the `onCreate` method. Instead, we can now check the `mIsDynamic` class-level field to determine the proper handling. With that in mind, we can initially modify the `onSelectedBookChanged` method to now look like the following code:

```
public void onSelectedBookChanged(int bookIndex) {
  BookDescFragment bookDescFragment;
  FragmentManager fm = getFragmentManager();

  // Check validity of fragment reference
  if(mIsDynamic)
    // Handle dynamic switch to description fragment
  else {
    // Use the already visible description fragment
    bookDescFragment = (BookDescFragment)
        fm.findFragmentById(R.id.fragmentDescription);
    bookDescFragment.setBook(bookIndex);
  }
}
```

We now check the `mIsDynamic` member field to determine the appropriate code path. We still have some work to do if it turns out to be true, but in the case of it being false, we can simply get a reference to the book description fragment that we know is contained within the current layout and set the book index on it much like we were doing before.

Creating the fragment on-the-fly

In the case of the `mIsDynamic` field being true, we can display the book description fragment by simply replacing the book list fragment we added in the `onCreate` method with the book description fragment using the code shown here:

```
FragmentTransaction ft = fm.beginTransaction();
bookDescFragment = new BookDescFragment();
ft.replace(R.id.layoutRoot, bookDescFragment, "bookDescription");
ft.addToBackStack(null);
ft.setCustomAnimations(
    android.R.animator.fade_in, android.R.animator.fade_out);
ft.commit();
```

Within `FragmentTransaction` we create an instance of the `BookDescFragment` class and call the `replace` method passing the ID of the same view group that contains the `BookListFragment2` instance that we added in the `onCreate` method. We include a call to the `addToBackStack` method so that the back button functions correctly, allowing the user to tap the back button to return to the book list.

 The code includes a call to the `FragmentTransaction` class' `setCustomAnimations` method that creates a fade effect when the user switches from one fragment to the other.

Managing asynchronous creation

We have one final challenge, that is, setting the book index on the dynamically added book description fragment. Our initial thought might be to simply call the `BookDescFragment` class' `setBook` method after we create the `BookDescFragment` instance, but let's first take a look at the current implementation of the `setBook` method that appears as follows:

```
public void setBook(int bookIndex) {
    // Lookup the book description
    String bookDescription = mBookDescriptions[bookIndex];

    // Display it
    mBookDescriptionTextView.setText(bookDescription);
}
```

The last line of the method attempts to set the value of mBookDescriptionTextView within the fragment, which is a problem. Remember that the work we do within a FragmentTransaction class is not immediately applied to the user interface, but is instead performed only after we call the commit method. As a result, the BookDescFragment instance's onCreate and onCreateView methods have not yet been called. Therefore, any views associated with the BookDescFragment instance have not yet been created. An attempt to call the setText method on the mBookDescriptionTextView instance would result in a null reference exception.

One possible solution would be to modify the setBook method to be aware of the current state of the fragment. In that scenario, the setBook method would check whether the BookDescFragment instance had been fully created. If not, it would store the book index value in the class-level field and later automatically set the mBookDescriptionTextView value as part of the creation process. Although there may be some scenarios that warrant such a complicated solution, fragments give us an easier one.

The Fragment base class includes a method called setArguments. With the setArguments method, we can attach data values, otherwise known as arguments, to the fragment that can then be accessed later in the fragment lifecycle using the getArguments method. Much like we do when associating extras with an Intent instance, a good practice is to define constants on the target class to name the argument values. It is also a good programming practice to provide a constant for an argument default value in the case of non-nullable types such as integers as shown here:

```
public class BookDescFragment extends Fragment {
    // Book index argument name
    public static final String BOOK_INDEX = "book index";
    // Book index default value
    private static final int BOOK_INDEX_NOT_SET = -1;

    // Other members elided for clarity
}
```

We'll use the BOOK_INDEX constant to get and set the book index value and the BOOK_INDEX_NOT_SET constant to indicate whether the book index argument has been set.

We can now update the `BookDescFragment` class' `onCreateView` method to look for arguments that might be attached to the fragment. Before we make any changes to the `onCreateView` method, let's look at the current implementation that follows:

```
public View onCreateView(LayoutInflater inflater,
    ViewGroup container, Bundle savedInstanceState) {
  View viewHierarchy = inflater.inflate(
      R.layout.fragment_book_desc, container, false);

  // Load array of book descriptions
  mBookDescriptions =
      getResources().getStringArray(R.array.bookDescriptions);
  // Get reference to book description text view
  mBookDescriptionTextView = (TextView)
      viewHierarchy.findViewById(R.id.bookDescription);

  return viewHierarchy;
}
```

As the `onCreateView` method is currently implemented, it simply inflates the layout resource, loads the array containing the book descriptions, and caches a reference to the `TextView` instance where the book description is loaded.

We can now update the method to look for and use a book index that might be attached as an argument. The updated method appears as follows:

```
public View onCreateView(LayoutInflater inflater,
    ViewGroup container, Bundle savedInstanceState) {
  View viewHierarchy = inflater.inflate(
      R.layout.fragment_book_desc, container, false);

  // Load array of book descriptions
  mBookDescriptions =
      getResources().getStringArray(R.array.bookDescriptions);
  // Get reference to book description text view
  mBookDescriptionTextView = (TextView)
      viewHierarchy.findViewById(R.id.bookDescription);

  // Retrieve the book index if attached
  Bundle args = getArguments();
  int bookIndex = args != null ?
      args.getInt(BOOK_INDEX, BOOK_INDEX_NOT_SET) :
      BOOK_INDEX_NOT_SET;

  // If we find the book index, use it
```

```
    if (bookIndex != BOOK_INDEX_NOT_SET)
      setBook(bookIndex);

    return viewHierarchy;
  }
```

Just before we return the fragment's view hierarchy, we call the `getArguments` method to retrieve any arguments that might be attached. The arguments are returned as an instance of the `Bundle` class. If the `Bundle` instance is non-null, we call the `Bundle` class' `getInt` method to retrieve the book index and assign it the `bookIndex` local variable. The second parameter to the `getInt` method, `BOOK_INDEX_NOT_SET`, is returned if the fragment happens to have arguments attached that do not include the book index. Although this should not normally be the case, being prepared for any such unexpected circumstance is a good idea. Finally, we check the value of the `bookIndex` variable. If it contains a book index, we call the fragment's `setBook` method to display it.

Putting it all together

With the `BookDescFragment` class now including support for attaching the book index as an argument, we're ready to fully implement the main activity's `onSelectedBookChanged` method to include switching to the `BookDescFragment` instance and attaching the book index as an argument. The method now appears as follows:

```
public void onSelectedBookChanged(int bookIndex) {
  BookDescFragment bookDescFragment;
  FragmentManager fm = getFragmentManager();

  // Check validity of fragment reference
  if(mIsDynamic){
    // Handle dynamic switch to description fragment
    FragmentTransaction ft = fm.beginTransaction();

    // Create the fragment and attach book index
    bookDescFragment = new BookDescFragment();
    Bundle args = new Bundle();
    args.putInt(BookDescFragment.BOOK_INDEX, bookIndex);
    bookDescFragment.setArguments(args);

    // Replace the book list with the description
    ft.replace(R.id.layoutRoot,
        bookDescFragment, "bookDescription");
    ft.addToBackStack(null);
```

```
        ft.setCustomAnimations(
            android.R.animator.fade_in, android.R.animator.fade_out);
        ft.commit();
    }
    else {
      // Use the already visible description fragment
      bookDescFragment = (BookDescFragment)
          fm.findFragmentById(R.id.fragmentDescription);
      bookDescFragment.setBook(bookIndex);
    }
}
```

Just as before, we start with the check to see if we're doing dynamic fragment management. Once we determine we are, we start the FragmentTransaction instance and create the BookDescFragment instance. We then create a new Bundle instance, store the book index into it, and then attach the Bundle instance to the BookDescFragment instance with the setArguments method. Finally, we put the BookDescFragment instance into place as the current fragment, take care of the back stack, enable animation, and complete the transaction.

Everything is now complete. When the user selects a book title from the list, the onSelectedBookChanged method gets called. The onSelectedBookChanged method then creates and displays the BookDescFragment instance with the appropriate book index attached as an argument. When the BookDescFragment instance is ultimately created, its onCreateView method will then retrieve the book index from the arguments and display the appropriate description.

Summary

Intentional screen management frees us from the burden of tying each application screen to an individual activity. Using the FragmentTransaction class, we're able to dynamically switch between individual fragments within an activity, eliminating the need to create a separate activity class for each screen in our application. This helps to prevent the proliferation of unnecessary activity classes, better organize our applications, and avoid the associated increase in complexity.

We'll see in the next chapter that this ability to dynamically manage multiple screens within a single activity opens us up to greater flexibility and an increased richness in the appearance and navigation behavior of our Android applications.

5

Creating Rich Navigation with Fragments

This chapter demonstrates the role of fragments in creating a rich user interface navigation experience.

The following topics are covered in this chapter:

- Swipe navigation
- The role of the Android action bar
- The close relationship between the action bar and fragments
- Associating menus with fragments
- List navigation
- Tab navigation

By the end of this chapter, we will be able to implement solutions that utilize fragments to provide rich user navigation, including swipe navigation, tab navigation, and drop-down list navigation.

A brave new world

As we've seen, fragments provide us with the ability to closely control and manage our application user interface. Through the use of the `FragmentTransaction` class we can provide the user with the experience of moving from one screen to another by simply switching between different fragments. This takes us to an entirely new way of thinking: a brave new world of application design.

When we create our user interface in this way, the activity acts as a sort of screen manager with the fragments implementing the screens themselves. This concept of managing the individual application screens as fragments within an activity is so powerful that it has become the foundation of some of the most compelling navigation features of the Android platform.

Android provides classes that cooperate with this design pattern to enable us to create rich navigation and screen management experiences, in a simple way. These classes provide a variety of features, including transition effects along with some familiar user interface metaphors.

Making navigation fun with swipe

Many applications involve several screens of data that a user might want to browse or flip through to view each screen. As an example, think of an application where we list a catalogue of books with each book in the catalogue appearing on a single screen. A book's screen contains an image, title, and description like the following screenshot:

To view each book's information, the user needs to move to each screen. We could put a next button and a previous button on the screen, but a more natural action is for the user to use their thumb or finger to swipe the screen from one edge of the display to the other and have the screen with the next book's information slide into place as represented in the following screenshot:

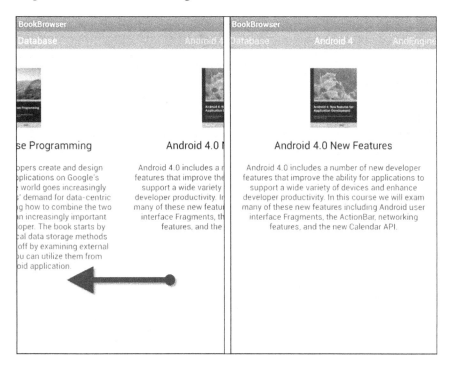

This creates a very natural navigation experience, and honestly, is a more fun way to navigate through an application than using buttons.

Implementing swipe navigation

Implementing swipe navigation is pretty simple, and fragments are at the core. Each of the screens is implemented as a fragment derived class. Each screen can be a completely different fragment derived class or the screens can be instances of the same fragment derived class with different data. To create a book browser app such as the one shown in the previous screenshot, we can use a simple fragment derived class that sets the book image, title, and description.

There is one thing about the fragment derived class that is a bit unusual. At the time of this writing, the classes involved in managing swipe navigation are relatively new and are only available in the android.support.v4.app package. As a result, the fragment derived class created by us must inherit from the support package version of the Fragment class, android.support.v4.app.Fragment, even when our app is targeting the Android versions that natively support fragments. The fragment class definition will appear similar to the following code:

```
import android.support.v4.app.Fragment;
public class BookFragment extends Fragment {
  // members elided for clarity

}
```

Managing the swipe fragments

Presenting the individual fragments that represent the application screens requires an adapter to manage the creation and delivery of each fragment. The Android support library includes two classes that provide this capability: FragmentPagerAdapter and FragmentStatePagerAdapter.

The FragmentPagerAdapter class is useful for scenarios where there are a small number of fragments. When a given fragment instance is created, it is directly stored in the FragmentManager class and that same instance is re-used each time that fragment's page is displayed. The fragment's onDestroyView method is called when the user switches to a different fragment, but not the onDestroy method. It's important that we only use the FragmentPagerAdapter class in cases where there's a relatively small number of fragments, because we should assume that once a fragment is created, it will exist as long as the FragmentPagerAdapter class exists.

The `FragmentStatePagerAdapter` class is useful for scenarios where there is a large number of fragments, because fragments may be destroyed when they are no longer visible. Fragments managed by `FragmentStatePagerAdapter` will always have their `onDestroyView` method called, and may have their `onDestroy` method called as well. The call to the `onDestroy` method does not necessarily occur as soon as the user swipes to another fragment it may occur much later depending on the device's available resources. The `FragmentStatePagerAdapter` class gives the fragment an opportunity to save its state through the platform's call to the `onSaveInstanceState` method.

The ability to discard and recreate the contained fragments also makes the `FragmentStatePagerAdapter` class useful for scenarios where the list of fragments being displayed may change. The details of implementing an updatable `FragmentStatePagerAdapter` instance are beyond the scope of this book, but an example is available at `http://bit.ly/UpdateFragmentStatePagerAdapter`.

To create a book browser app as seen in the previous screenshot, we'll extend the `FragmentPagerAdapter` class because we'll be displaying just a few books. We'll name our class as `BookPagerAdapter`, the declaration of which is shown in the following code:

```
public class BookPagerAdapter extends FragmentPagerAdapter {
    // members elided for clarity
}
```

To implement our `BookPagerAdapter` class, we just need to override a few methods. The primary method, `getItem`, is responsible for returning each fragment instance. Our `getItem` method appears as follows:

```
public Fragment getItem(int idx) {

    // Store the argument values for this fragment
    Bundle arguments = new Bundle();
    arguments.putString(
        BookFragment.BOOK_TITLE, mCourseTitles[idx]);
    arguments.putString(
        BookFragment.BOOK_DESCRIPTIONS, mCourseDescriptions[idx]);
    arguments.putInt(
        BookFragment.TOP_IMAGE, mTopImageResourceIds[idx]);

    // Create the fragment instance and pass the arguments
    BookFragment bookFragment = new BookFragment();
    bookFragment.setArguments(arguments);

    // return the fragment instance
    return bookFragment;
}
```

When the app displays a particular book's page for the first time, the getItem method is called with the index of the page as a parameter named idx in our code. Before creating the fragment, we retrieve the book title, description, and image resource ID from arrays containing those values and store them in a Bundle instance. We then create an instance of our BookFragment class and associate the argument Bundle instance with it. Finally, we return the BookFragment reference. When our BookFragment instance is displayed, it will access the values in the argument Bundle instance and display them.

We now must override two additional methods: getPageTitle and getCount. The getPageTitle method returns the string that is visible in the thin bar above each fragment. Like the getItem method, the getPageTitle method receives the index of the page being displayed. The getPageTitle method simply returns a value from an array containing short versions of the page title, as shown in the following code:

```
public CharSequence getPageTitle(int idx) {
    return mCourseTitlesShort[idx];
}
```

The getCount method is responsible for returning the number of screens we'll be displaying. We can simply return the length of the array we're using in the getPageTitle method, as shown in the following code:

```
public int getCount() {
    return mCourseTitlesShort.length;
}
```

Implementing our BookPagerAdapter class takes care of the code that manages our fragments. Now, we just need to put the appropriate layout within our activity and connect it with the adapter.

Putting the swipe UI into place

The swipe user interface behavior and effects come from two Android classes: ViewPager and PagerTitleStrip. The ViewPager class is the primary class. It manages the user interaction, provides the swipe animation effects, and cooperates with the adapter class that provides each screen's fragment. The PagerTitleStrip class handles the displaying of the thin title bar above each fragment. The string values returned from our BookPagerAdapter class' getPageTitle method are displayed within the PagerTitleStrip instance.

We'll create a layout resource file for our application's activity called `activity_main.xml` containing the `ViewPager` and `PagerTitleStrip` classes, as shown in the following XML layout:

```xml
<android.support.v4.view.ViewPager
    xmlns:android="http://schemas.android.com/apk/res/android"
    android:id="@+id/pager"
    android:layout_width="match_parent"
    android:layout_height="match_parent">

    <android.support.v4.view.PagerTitleStrip
        android:id="@+id/pager_title_strip"
        android:layout_width="match_parent"
        android:layout_height="wrap_content"
        android:layout_gravity="top"
        android:background="#33b5e5"
        android:paddingBottom="4dp"
        android:paddingTop="4dp"
        android:textColor="#fff"/>

</android.support.v4.view.ViewPager>
```

Our layout resource file contains `ViewPager` as the root node, and is set to occupy the entire activity. The `ViewPager` class has an ID value of `pager`. The `PagerTitleStrip` class is set to fill the full width of `ViewPager`, and to be positioned at the top. Alternatively we could set the `layout_gravity` attribute to a value of `bottom` to position `PagerTitleStrip` at the bottom of the `ViewPager` class' display area. Although, other values for the `layout_gravity` attribute are technically valid, they tend to be problematic. As a general rule, we want to limit our choices for the `layout_gravity` attribute to be either `top` or `bottom`.

We have our complete layout and have already created the adapter that will manage the fragments within our application. We're now ready to declare our activity class, which we'll name `MainActivity`. The class declaration appears as follows:

```java
import android.support.v4.app.FragmentActivity;
import android.support.v4.view.ViewPager;

public class MainActivity extends FragmentActivity {
  BookPagerAdapter mBookPagerAdapter;
  ViewPager mViewPager;

  // other members elided for clarity
}
```

Notice that we're inheriting from the support library class `FragmentActvity` rather than the regular `Activity` class. This is due to the same issue we discussed when we declared our `BookFragment` class. The classes that provide the swipe behavior are in the support library; therefore, they expect all fragment-related classes to be from that library. Our activity class includes member variables for our `BookPagerAdapter` and `ViewPager` classes.

The last thing we need to do is connect our `BookPagerAdapter` class to the `ViewPager` class. We'll do that in our `onCreate` method, which appears as follows:

```
protected void onCreate(Bundle savedInstanceState) {
    super.onCreate(savedInstanceState);
    setContentView(R.layout.activity_main);

    mBookPagerAdapter = new BookPagerAdapter(
        getSupportFragmentManager(), this);

    mViewPager = (ViewPager) findViewById(R.id.pager);
    mViewPager.setAdapter(mBookPagerAdapter);
}
```

As we can see, our job here is pretty easy. We call the `setContentView` method with the `R.layout.activity_main` resource we just created. When the `setContentView` method returns, we create our `BookPagerAdapter` instance passing the activity's `FragmentManager` instance and the activity's `this` pointer so our `BookPagerAdapter` can use it as the context. With our `BookPagerAdapter` created, we use the activity class' `findViewById` method to get a reference to the `ViewPager` class that we created with the layout resource file. Finally, we call the `ViewPager` instance's `setAdapter` method to connect the `BookPagerAdapter` instance to our `ViewPager` instance.

We now have everything in place. Our book browser is all ready for the user to browse through our list of books using swipe navigation.

Android Studio and swipe navigation

If we're working with Android Studio, getting started at building an app with swipe navigation is easy. In the **New Project** wizard, on the dialog where we set the activity and layout name, select **Scrollable Tabs + Swipe** for **Navigation Type** as shown in the following screenshot:

The resulting project will include a layout resource file containing ViewPager and PagerTitleStrip, along with stubbed-out code for the FragmentPagerAdapter, Fragment, and Activity derived classes.

Improving navigation with the ActionBar

Beginning at API Level 11 (Android 3.0), Android moved away from using traditional menus to instead use the ActionBar. The ActionBar provides action items that are a combination of button-based actions that appear directly on the ActionBar and menu-based actions that appear in a drop-down list when the user taps on the Action overflow button. The following screenshot shows the available ActionBar actions:

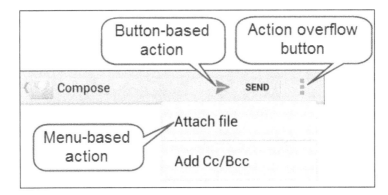

What many developers don't realize is that the button-based and menu-based actions are just a small subset of what the ActionBar actually does. The ActionBar now serves as a central point for many navigation-related behaviors. Two of these behaviors are tied directly to fragments: tab navigation and drop-down navigation.

To incorporate the ActionBar in applications targeting versions of Android with an API Level below 11, use the ActionBarCompat class available in the Android Support Library. For more information on the ActionBarCompat class visit http://bit.ly/ActionBarCompat.

Navigating randomly with tabs

Tabs are an effective navigation model. They're well understood by users, and make moving between screens within an app easy. Unlike swipe navigation that requires the user to move through screens in order, tab navigation allows the user to move from one screen to another in any order they like. Android has supported tab navigation since the original release of the platform. Historically, the challenge of implementing tab navigation was that it was unrelated to other navigation models and required using a special activity class and other tab-specific classes. With the ActionBar, this is all changed. Now, tab navigation is just another use of the common fragment programming model.

The ActionBar allows us to associate an instance of a fragment derived class with each tab. The following screenshot shows the top portion of the screen of two different devices, with the ActionBar displaying tabs:

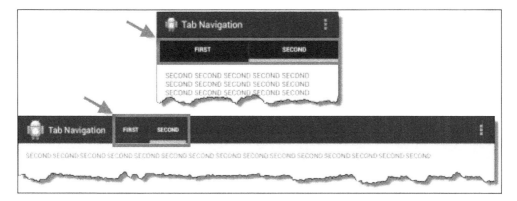

Notice that the ActionBar automatically adapts the way the tabs are displayed in response to the available screen space. On the narrower device, the ActionBar places the tabs under the main portion of the ActionBar, whereas on the wider device with more horizontal screen space, the tabs appear directly on the main portion of the ActionBar.

Managing tab selection

The ActionBar manages all the heavy lifting when it comes to implementing tab navigation. It draws the tabs, indicates which tab is currently selected, and even takes care of beginning and committing a fragment transaction. All we have to do is handle which fragment is visible, based on the tab currently selected. We do this by providing an implementation of the `ActionBar.TabListener` interface for each tab. The following code shows the declaration of a class implementing the interface:

```
public class SimpleTabListener implements ActionBar.TabListener {
  boolean mFirstSelect = true;
  Fragment mFragment;

  public SimpleTabListener(Fragment fragment) {
    mFragment = fragment;
  }

  // Other members elided for clarity
}
```

Our `TabListener` implementation has two member variables. The boolean member variable, `mFirstSelect`, is used to control the special handling that's necessary the first time the fragment managed by our `SimpleTabListener` class is selected. The other member variable, `mFragment`, holds a reference to the fragment that is managed by the `TabListener` instance, which is set in our `SimpleTabListener` constructor.

The first `TabListener` interface method we'll implement is the `onTabSelected` method. As the method name indicates, `onTabSelected` is called each time the tab associated with this `TabListener` instance becomes the selected tab. The `onTabSelected` method is implemented as shown in the following code:

```
public void onTabSelected(
    ActionBar.Tab tab, FragmentTransaction fragmentTransaction) {
  if (mFirstSelect) {
    fragmentTransaction.add(android.R.id.content, mFragment);
    mFirstSelect = false;
  }
  else
    fragmentTransaction.attach(mFragment);
}
```

Two parameters are passed to the `onTabSelected` method. The first parameter is a reference to the tab instance that is associated with our `TabListener` implementation. The second parameter is the `FragmentTransaction` instance that is managed by the ActionBar. The ActionBar starts this transaction, and will commit the transaction after `onTabSelected` returns.

The first time the `onTabSelected` method is called, we use the passed `FragmentTransaction` instance to add our fragment to the display using the `add` method. As we discussed in the previous chapter, the first parameter to the `add` method is the ID of the view group under which we want the fragment to be placed. Just as when we're managing `FragmentsTransaction` ourselves, this can be any valid view group within the activity layout. In the previous code, we're using a special ID value that is predefined by Android, `android.R.id.content`. The `android.R.id.content` ID value indicates that we want the fragment to occupy the entire content area of the activity rather than be placed under a specific view group within the activity.

We only use the `add` method the first time the tab is selected; every time thereafter, we use the `FragmentTransaction` class' `attach` method. We'll talk more about that in a moment.

The next `TabListener` interface method we'll implement is the `onTabUnselected` method, which is shown in the following code:

```
public void onTabUnselected(
    ActionBar.Tab tab, FragmentTransaction fragmentTransaction) {
  fragmentTransaction.detach(mFragment);
}
```

The `onTabUnselected` method receives the same parameters as the `onTabSelected` method. Our implementation of this method is simple, having only one line in which we call the `FragmentTransaction` class' `detach` method.

The `detach` method call in the `onTabUnselected` method works together with the `attach` method call in the `onTabSelected` method. Once the fragment is initially added to the activity, as we do in the `onTabSelected` method the first time the fragment is shown, we can then call the `detach` method to tear down the fragment's view hierarchy, but leave the fragment associated with the activity. When we call the `attach` method within the `onTabSelected` method, the next time the user selects the tab for the fragment, the fragment's view hierarchy is rebuilt at the same place within the activity where the fragment was originally added.

This technique of calling the `detach` and `attach` methods allows us to manage the fragments more efficiently. When we call the `detach` method, the fragment's `onDestroyView` method is called, but not the `onDestroy` method. When we later call the `attach` method, the fragment's `onCreateView` method is called, but not the `onCreate` method, because the fragment does not need to be fully recreated just its view hierarchy needs to be recreated.

There is a bit of potential confusion related to method names that we need to be aware of. When a fragment instance is passed to the `FragmentTransaction` class' `detach` method, the `Fragment` class' `onDetach` method does not get called. This is because the `detach` method tears down the fragment's view hierarchy but leaves the fragment associated with the activity; the fragment remains attached. Similarly, when a fragment instance is passed to the `FragmentTransaction` class' `attach` method, the `Fragment` class' `onAttach` method does not get called because the fragment is already attached to the activity. This is certainly a little confusing, but it ultimately comes down to a bad choice of method names on the part of the API designers rather than being a technical inconsistency.

The last method on the TabListener interface, onTabReselected, is called in scenarios where the user taps the tab that is already selected; in other words, the user reselects the same tab. In most cases, this method can be left empty, as shown in the following code:

```
public void onTabReselected(
    ActionBar.Tab tab, FragmentTransaction fragmentTransaction) { }
```

Connecting the fragments to the tabs

With our TabListener implementation in place, we can now connect the fragments to the tabs. We'll do this in the activity's onCreate method, which is shown in the following code:

```
protected void onCreate(Bundle savedInstanceState) {
    super.onCreate(savedInstanceState);

    // Put ActionBar in Tab mode
    ActionBar actionBar = getActionBar();
    actionBar.setNavigationMode(ActionBar.NAVIGATION_MODE_TABS);

    // Create the first tab
    Fragment firstFragment = new FirstFragment();
    ActionBar.TabListener firstListener =
        new SimpleTabListener(firstFragment);
    ActionBar.Tab firstTab = actionBar.newTab()
        .setText("First")
        .setTabListener(firstListener);
    actionBar.addTab(firstTab);

    // Create the second tab
    Fragment secondFragment = new SecondFragment();
    ActionBar.TabListener secondListener =
        new SimpleTabListener(secondFragment);
    ActionBar.Tab secondTab = actionBar.newTab()
        .setText("Second")
        .setTabListener(secondListener);
    actionBar.addTab(secondTab);
}
```

In our onCreate implementation, we start by getting a reference to the ActionBar, and putting the ActionBar into tab navigation mode. This step is essential; without it, the tabs we add will never be visible.

For the first tab, we create the fragment that will serve as the body of the tab. This can be virtually any fragment derived class. We then associate our `TabListener` implementation with the fragment. With the fragment and `TabListener` implementation in place, we create a new `ActionBar.Tab` instance with the call to the `newTab` method, we then set the text that will display within the tab, and associate our `TabListener` instance with the tab. Finally, we add the `ActionBar.Tab` instance to the ActionBar with the `addTab` method. We then repeat those steps for the second tab.

With that, we now have tab navigation implemented in our application. Using this technique, we're able to leverage all the capabilities of fragments and implement tab-based navigation in a way that is consistent with other ways we use fragments.

One thing that may appear unusual about our `onCreate` method implementation is the absence of a call to the `setContentView` method. In this case, we don't need to associate a layout resource with the activity, because we're using the special-purpose `android.R.id.content` resource ID when we call the `add` method in our `onTabSelected` implementation. As we mentioned earlier, the resource ID `android.R.id.content` indicates that the fragment occupies the entire content area. If we wanted the tab to control the display of a fragment within some view group, we would call `setContentView` with a resource containing the desired layout. We would then use the ID of the view group within that layout in our call to the `add` method.

Providing direct access with drop-down list navigation

Tab navigation works well when an app has just a few predictable screens, but quickly becomes cluttered if there are a large number of screens. For those scenarios where an app has a large number of screens or possibly the number of screens might even change over time, drop-down list navigation provides a much better solution than tabs. Drop-down list navigation places a drop-down list on the ActionBar containing the list of available screen names. When the user chooses a screen name from the list, the app immediately displays the corresponding screen.

Probably the most familiar use of this navigation model on Android is the Android e-mail app, which is shown in the following screenshot:

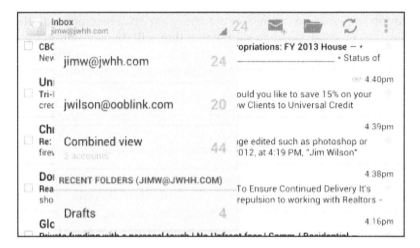

In the Android e-mail app, the list of different available e-mail folder screens appears in the drop-down list. Tapping the ActionBar displays the list and then selecting the screen name from the list immediately displays the screen.

Incorporating drop-down list navigation in our apps is very simple.

Managing fragment selection

Unlike tab navigation, where the ActionBar takes a very active role in managing the transition from one fragment to another, in drop-down list navigation the ActionBar takes a much more hands-off approach. Basically, the ActionBar simply notifies the app that the selection has changed, and leaves the details of switching fragments up to the app. To handle the notification we need to provide an implementation of the ActionBar.OnNavigationListener interface. The implementation declaration is shown in the following code:

```
public class SimpleNavigationListener
    implements ActionBar.OnNavigationListener {
  FragmentManager mFragmentManager;

  public SimpleNavigationListener(FragmentManager fm) {
    mFragmentManager = fm;
  }

  // Other members elided for clarity
}
```

Our `ActionBar.OnNavigationListener` implementation has a single member variable, `mFragmentManager`, to hold a reference to the activity's `FragmentManager` instance. The `FragmentManager` reference is passed to our class in the constructor.

Unlike in tab navigation where each tab instance is managed by a separate `TabListener` instance, in drop-down list navigation a single `OnNavigationListener` implementation handles all the selections. The `OnNavigationListener` interface's only method, `onNavigationItemSelected`, is called each time the selection changes and is responsible for taking care of displaying the appropriate fragment, as shown in the following implementation:

```
public boolean onNavigationItemSelected(
    int itemPosition, long itemId) {
  Fragment fragment = null;

  // Create an instance of the appropriate Fragment
  switch (itemPosition) {
    case 0:
      fragment = new FirstFragment();
      break;
    case 1:
      fragment = new SecondFragment();
      break;
    case 2:
      fragment = new ThirdFragment();
      break;
  }

  // Replace the currently visible fragment with the new one
  if (fragment != null) {
    FragmentTransaction ft = mFragmentManager.beginTransaction();
    ft.replace(android.R.id.content, fragment);
    ft.commit();
  }

  return true;
}
```

We receive the zero-based index of the selection as the first parameter, `itemPosition`. We'll be populating the list of screen names from a simple `String` array so the second parameter, `itemId`, does not have value to us. If we were to use a more structured data source, the `itemId` parameter would contain the ID of the selection.

Using a `switch` statement, we create an instance of the appropriate fragment derived class. Once we have the fragment instance, we replace the currently visible fragment with the one we just created. We again use the layout resource ID, `android.R.id.content`, indicating that the fragment occupies the entire content area of the activity. Just as with tab navigation, we could instead use the ID value of a view group within the activity's layout, if we prefer.

Notice that we're explicitly creating and committing the `FragmentTransaction` instance in our code. This is another important difference from how tab navigation is managed; we're responsible for all the details. The test that the local variable, `fragment`, is not null is just a sanity check. As long as we don't display more than three values for the user to select from, the `fragment` variable will never be null.

Providing a method return value of `true` simply indicates that we have handled the event.

Providing the navigation choices

We now need to provide the ActionBar with the information necessary to display the list of navigation choices. We do that in the activity's `onCreate` method, which is shown in the following code:

```
protected void onCreate(Bundle savedInstanceState) {
  super.onCreate(savedInstanceState);

  // Put the ActionBar in the right mode and clear any clutter
  ActionBar actionBar = getActionBar();
  actionBar.setNavigationMode(ActionBar.NAVIGATION_MODE_LIST);
  actionBar.setDisplayShowTitleEnabled(false);

  // Get the list of display values and wrap in an adapter
  String[] screenNames =
      getResources().getStringArray(R.array.screen_names);
  ArrayAdapter<String> adapter = new ArrayAdapter<String>(this,
      android.R.layout.simple_list_item_1, screenNames);

  // Create the Listener and associate with the ActionBar
  ActionBar.OnNavigationListener listener =
      new SimpleNavigationListener(getFragmentManager());
  actionBar.setListNavigationCallbacks(adapter, listener);
}
```

The first step in setting up drop-down list navigation is to put the ActionBar into list navigation mode with the call to the `setNavigationMode` method. The drop-down list containing the screen choices appears directly on the ActionBar, which can be problematic if the ActionBar attempts to show both the drop-down list and the activity title text. To make room for the list, we call the `setDisplayShowTitleEnabled` method with a value of `false` so that the title doesn't display.

We retrieve the list of display values from the array resource, which is a regular `String` array. We wrap the `String` array in an instance of the `ArrayAdapter` class just as we would if we were planning to associate the `String` array with a standard `ListView` instance appearing within a layout definition for an activity. The `String` array resource definition appears as shown in the following XML code:

```xml
<string-array name="screen_names">
  <item>First View</item>
  <item>Second View</item>
  <item>Third View</item>
</string-array>
```

We then create an instance of `SimpleNavigationListener`, which we had defined earlier. Finally, we set the list of displayed screen names and the screen selection handler by calling the `setListNavigationCallbacks` method to associate the `ArrayAdapter` and `SimpleNavigationListener` implementations with the `ActionBar`.

With that we have drop-down navigation fully implemented. When we run the application, the list of screen selections will appear as shown in the following screenshot. The ActionBar initially appears as shown on the left-hand side in the following screenshot, with the currently selected screen's name displayed. When the user taps on the currently selected screen name, the list expands to display the list of available screen names as shown on the right-hand side of the following screenshot. With the list expanded, the user can easily jump directly to any of the available screens by tapping on the desired screen's name within the list.

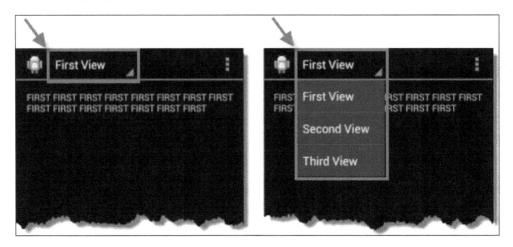

Android Studio and drop-down list navigation

If we're working with Android Studio, we can create a project that supports drop-down list navigation directly from the **New Project** wizard by selecting **Dropdown** as the **Navigation Type**, similar to the way we created a project with swipe navigation. The resulting project will contain a stubbed-out `ActionBar.OnNavigationListener` implementation along with the code within the activity to put the ActionBar into drop-down list navigation mode, and associate the `ActionBar.OnNavigationListener` implementation with the ActionBar.

Summary

Fragments are the foundation of modern Android app development, allowing us to display multiple application screens within a single activity. Thanks to the flexibility provided by fragments, we can now incorporate rich navigation into our apps with relative ease. Using these rich navigation capabilities, we're able to create a more dynamic user interface experience that make our apps more compelling and that users find more fun to work with.

Index

swipe UI, placing 86-88
switch statement 98

T

TabListener interface 94
TabListener interface method 92, 93
tabs
  fragments, connecting to 94, 95
  managing 91
  navigating with 90, 91
TextView element 10
TextView instance 78
tools:layout attribute 18
transaction changes
  executing 65, 66

U

UI creation
  need for 5, 6
UI flexibility
  creating 19, 20
  fragment layout 20, 21
  fragments, designing for flexibility 30

V

ViewGroup instance 15
View.OnClickListener interface 52, 56
ViewPager class 86-88
ViewPager instance 88

Thank you for buying
Creating Dynamic UI with Android Fragments

About Packt Publishing

Packt, pronounced 'packed', published its first book "*Mastering phpMyAdmin for Effective MySQL Management*" in April 2004 and subsequently continued to specialize in publishing highly focused books on specific technologies and solutions.

Our books and publications share the experiences of your fellow IT professionals in adapting and customizing today's systems, applications, and frameworks. Our solution based books give you the knowledge and power to customize the software and technologies you're using to get the job done. Packt books are more specific and less general than the IT books you have seen in the past. Our unique business model allows us to bring you more focused information, giving you more of what you need to know, and less of what you don't.

Packt is a modern, yet unique publishing company, which focuses on producing quality, cutting-edge books for communities of developers, administrators, and newbies alike. For more information, please visit our website: www.packtpub.com.

About Packt Open Source

In 2010, Packt launched two new brands, Packt Open Source and Packt Enterprise, in order to continue its focus on specialization. This book is part of the Packt Open Source brand, home to books published on software built around Open Source licences, and offering information to anybody from advanced developers to budding web designers. The Open Source brand also runs Packt's Open Source Royalty Scheme, by which Packt gives a royalty to each Open Source project about whose software a book is sold.

Writing for Packt

We welcome all inquiries from people who are interested in authoring. Book proposals should be sent to author@packtpub.com. If your book idea is still at an early stage and you would like to discuss it first before writing a formal book proposal, contact us; one of our commissioning editors will get in touch with you.

We're not just looking for published authors; if you have strong technical skills but no writing experience, our experienced editors can help you develop a writing career, or simply get some additional reward for your expertise.

Android User Interface Development: Beginner's Guide

ISBN: 978-1-84951-448-4   Paperback: 304 pages

Quickly design and develop compelling user interfaces for your Android applications

1. Leverage the Android platform's flexibility and power to design impactful user-interfaces

2. Build compelling, user-friendly applications that will look great on any Android device

3. Make your application stand out from the rest with styles and themes

4. A practical Beginner's Guide to take you step-by-step through the process of developing user interfaces to get your applications noticed!

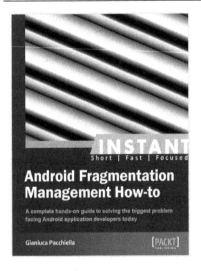

Instant Android Fragmentation Management How-to

ISBN: 978-1-78216-086-1   Paperback: 66 pages

A complete hands-on guide to solving the biggest problem facing Android application developers today

1. Learn something new in an Instant! A short, fast, focused guide delivering immediate results.

2. Learn how to write apps that work on any Android version

3. Ready to use code to solve any compatibility issue

4. Get hands-on with the biggest issue that faces Android developers

Please check **www.PacktPub.com** for information on our titles

Android 4: New Features for Application Development

ISBN: 978-1-84951-952-6   Paperback: 166 pages

Develop Android applications using the new features of Android Ice Cream Sandwich

1. Learn new APIs in Android 4

2. Get familiar with the best practices in developing Android applications

3. Step-by-step approach with clearly explained sample codes

Android 3.0 Application Development Cookbook

ISBN: 978-1-84951-294-7   Paperback: 272 pages

Over 70 working recipes covering every aspect of Android development

1. Written for Android 3.0 but also applicable to lower versions

2. Quickly develop applications that take advantage of the very latest mobile technologies, including web apps, sensors, and touch screens

4. Part of Packt's Cookbook series: Discover tips and tricks for varied and imaginative uses of the latest Android features

Please check **www.PacktPub.com** for information on our titles

www.ingramcontent.com/pod-product-compliance
Lightning Source LLC
Chambersburg PA
CBHW060155060326
40690CB00018B/4126